The Second Time Around

The Second Time Around

*Everything You Need to Know
to Make Your Remarriage Happy*

SUSAN KELLEY
AND DALE BURG

William Morrow
An Imprint of HarperCollins*Publishers*

HarperCollins books may be purchased for educational, business, or sales promotional use. For information please write: Special Markets Department, HarperCollins Publishers Inc., 10 East 53rd Street, New York, NY 10022.

FIRST EDITION

Designed by Bernard Klein

Printed on acid-free paper

Library of Congress Cataloging-in-Publication Data has been applied for.

ISBN 0-688-16651-2

00 01 02 03 04 FF 10 9 8 7 6 5 4 3 2 1

For Timothy and Molly; and for William, who came along when I had long since stopped expecting him and who has shown me the secret to a successful remarriage.

—Susan

For Richard and Alden.

—Dale

CONTENTS

ACKNOWLEDGMENTS

The authors are very grateful for the kindness of many people whose contributions were so significant to this book.

To Jill Sukenick, CSW; Roxanne Permesly, M.Ed., FMH, and LMHC; Scott Permesly, M.D.; Arthur D. Ginsburg, Esq.; Holli Bodner, Psy.D.; and Audrey Wentworth, LCSW, our profound gratitude for the many hours of time you spent with us and especially for your illuminating observations regarding relationships and remarriage.

To Karen Connery, Ph.D., Ruth Durschlag, Ph.D., Judith Peck, M.S.W., Joan Massel Soncini, Ph.D., and Judith Siegel, Ph.D., many thanks for your insightful comments.

To Paul Weinstein, much appreciation for leading us to Margaret Mead's *Male and Female.*

Thanks also to Pam Bernstein, our agent, for instantly seeing the merit in this project, and to editor Betty Kelly for sharing our enthusiasm.

Finally, and in a most heartfelt way, a special tribute to the many men and women who inspired us by having the courage to give romance another chance and who share their stories in these pages with candor, thoughtfulness, and eloquence.

PROLOGUE: WHY PEOPLE REMARRY

Since Western civilization began, the institution of marriage, while generally revered and respected, has also inspired a certain amount of knowing cynicism. Way back in 292 B.C., the Greek poet and dramatist Menander called it "an evil, but a necessary evil." In his great novel *Don Quixote,* Cervantes referred to marriage as a "noose." A century ago, Robert Louis Stevenson expressed the bleak notion that when you marry, you've come to the end of the road: "There are no more bypath meadows where you may innocently linger, but the road lies long and straight and dusty to the grave."

Times have changed. Even though one marriage in two ends in divorce, it seems that most people don't abandon the institution itself. For the last half century, although large numbers of people have opted to stray off the "long and straight and dusty" road of marriage to gambol in the meadows, such dalliances have often resulted in a return to the straight and dusty roads of wedlock.

Why? What does the straight and dusty road offer that gambols in the meadow do not? That question is the basis of this book.

Though the U.S. Census Bureau has stopped providing divorce and remarriage rates except at ten-year intervals, we can assume that the results of the 1990 census will soon be reaffirmed. The results of the 1990 survey suggest that three-quarters of divorced people will marry again. So will many widows and widowers. In fact, over 40 percent of all marriages are remarriages for one of the adults involved. This tendency to remarry has been noted by philosophers and poets for centuries. In 1595, the French writer Montaigne compared marriage to a cage: "The birds without despair to get in, and those within despair of getting out." Ralph Waldo Emerson echoed his sentiments in 1850 with almost the same words. "Such as are in the institution wish to get out, and such as are out wish to get in."

In an often-quoted aphorism, Samuel Johnson made much the same point. Remarking on the news that an unhappily wed man had re-married immediately after the death of his wife, Johnson called it "the triumph of hope over experience."

Whatever the statistics reveal, and no matter what the cynics say, most people seem to prefer being married to being single.

Although the tendency to remarry endures and, in fact, seems to be growing, there is not much material on the subject. A fair number of books deal with the problems of remarriage—particularly stepparenting and financial issues—but material about the nature of remarriage itself is scarce.

Statistics on the success of remarriage aren't cheering. Remarried people divorce at the same (or higher) rate than people in a first marriage do. Yet we personally know of many, many people who are in extremely happy second marriages, who have found in their second marriages what they failed to find in the first: lasting love, warm companionship, mutual compatibility, and satisfying sex. We wondered how a remarriage is different from the marriage that preceded it, and why? What makes one happier than another? We wanted people who were in successful second marriages to tell us what it was that made the remarriages work.

To find out, we surveyed hundreds of currently remarried men and women chosen at random from all over the United States. They ranged in age from 24 to nearly 80. The average age of a woman at her first marriage was 23, and her marriage lasted an average of 17 years. For 87 percent the first marriage ended in divorce, and for 13 percent it ended in death. At remarriage, the woman's average age was 40, and, at the time we conducted interviews, the remarriage had lasted for an average of 12.4 years. The men we surveyed averaged 26 years of age at the start of their first marriage, and remained in the marriage 12.8 years. For 90.9 percent it ended in divorce, and for 9.1 percent, in death. The men averaged 46.7 years of age at the start of their second marriage, which had lasted an average of 12.4 years.

Some of the men and women in the survey were interviewed personally, and others responded to solicitations to answer our questionnaire on the Internet. We did not screen out those people who were in an unhappy second marriage; indeed, most people who responded were those from whom we wanted to hear—people who were in successful marriages.

Here's who they were.

Age	Women	Men
25 or under	<1.0%	0
26–35	7.3%	2.2%
36–45	24.2%	6.5%
46–55	28.3%	37.0%
56–65	28.8%	32.6%
66+	11.4%	21.7%

The overwhelming majority of the people we surveyed—approximately 79 percent of both men and women—were in a second marriage; 10.7 percent of the women and 13.6 of the men, respectively, were in a third; and 3.1 and 7.4 percent, respectively, were in a fourth. None of the men, and 7.2 percent of the women, were in marriages that were a first for them and a remarriage for their spouse.

We asked them what they did right:

- How they put closure on the first marriage and decided to move forward;
- What changes they made in themselves or their circumstances before they considered remarriage;
- How they went about finding a more suitable partner;
- What criteria they used in choosing the new partner;
- How they dealt with the most problematic issues, such as former spouses, finances, and stepchildren;
- And, finally, what they thought made remarriages succeed.

We were encouraged by one surprising finding. When asked "Are you happier now in your current marriage than you were in your previous marriage?" over 89 percent of the women and 94 percent of respondents answered yes. The very few exceptions were almost all living with a partner who had serious alcohol or other abuse issues. Even when there were other concerns—including problems with finances, stepparenting, in-laws, former spouses, sex, or even "I can't *stand* his dogs!"—remarried people overwhelmingly felt that their current marriages were better than the ones that had preceded them.

But why?

Are expectations for a second marriage different? Is the tolerance level higher? Do people develop more skills in problem-solving? Or do people simply tend to choose a more appropriate partner in a second marriage? What, in short, can other people's happy remarriages teach us that can shape and strengthen our own marriages? These are some of the issues we explored, and this is what the book is about.

Any discussion of remarriage has as its background the issue of why the first marriage ended. Whether your marriage ended in death or divorce, you will have to deal with grief and closure; in the latter case, finding closure will be particularly complicated. Since religious and civil ceremonies both make the assumption that marriage vows are for life, it is almost inevitable that both parties will feel some shame when a marriage breaks apart. Like love and marriage, shame and blame usually work in tandem. Husband and wife may point fingers at one another to explain why the marriage "failed" but most also blame themselves. Even if they are justifiably angry, even if they are thoroughly convinced that divorce was the correct and perhaps only option, most divorced people at some point wonder if they were in any way at fault: If I had behaved differently, would the marriage have survived? For a variety of reasons, we can say that the answer is, Probably not.

Why divorce may be inevitable

One interesting way to lift some of the burden of responsibility is to consider the provocative theory that we are not meant to pair with one partner for life—despite what civil and religious ceremonies say, and no matter how much society cherishes this idea. The idea of a lifelong marriage may no longer be an appropriate model.

Conventional wisdom has it that people get married because they are in love. But defining love has always been a dicey business. In the thirteenth chapter of 1 Corinthians, Paul set down a definition for Christian marriage whose sentiments are also expressed in the marriage rites of Jews, Muslims, Hindus, Buddhists, and others:

> Love suffereth long, and is kind; love envieth not; love vaunteth not itself, is not puffed up, doth not behave itself unseemly, seeketh not her own, is not easily provoked, thinketh no evil; rejoiceth not in iniquity, but rejoiceth in the truth; beareth all things, believeth all things, hopeth all things, endureth all things.
>
> Love never faileth.

Unfortunately, this advice is like the information that you get in your computer manual—theoretically irreproachable, but not really helpful.

Most people seem to choose their partners for a first marriage as if they were just going to go on an extended date. The people we interviewed consistently reported that when they made their first marriages, they weren't looking far into the future. They "fell in love" with someone whom they found attractive, who met their general expectations for suitability, and whom they found compatible, socially and sexually.

In July 1991, *Cosmopolitan* magazine did a survey in which divorced women explained why they married their husbands: 96 percent cited love, and 84 percent mentioned security. The desire to have children and parental or peer pressure influenced 54 and 43 percent, respectively.

"First marriages," says Erica Abeel in her novel *Only When I Laugh,* "are all glands, fantasy, and fleeing your background." Her observation is as true as it is amusing. It wasn't clear in the *Cosmopolitan* survey whether people were thinking about emotional or financial security, but we suspect that the vast majority of those surveyed were thinking about the former. Of course the financial burden was once placed almost entirely on the man, but today men and women alike seem to expect that both marriage partners will shoulder a portion of the economic load.

With this one admittedly huge exception, things generally have not changed significantly in the fifty years since the great anthropologist Margaret Mead wrote her classic study about the sexes, *Male and Female.* What may be surprising to anyone not familiar with her work is the strong—and more timely than ever—argument she makes for the inevitability of divorce.

Mead wrote that "the American form of marriage is one of the most difficult that the human race has ever attempted." As she pointed out, we are expected to choose partners for life from an enormous, changing pool of prospects whose habits and social backgrounds may be very different from our own. These candidates don't have to pass any kind of qualifying test, nor do they have to receive any kind of counseling, go through administrative barriers to secure a license (although, in fact, a proposal for a matrimonial waiting period, modeled on gun-control law, has been put forth), or even prove that they are not saddled with health, mental, or legal problems. We are free to marry whoever we choose, without the consent or approval of our parents or anyone else.

Finally, we're supposed to select this person for a very long-term position for which no job description exists. Marriage is unique among human enterprises in that it assumes a fifty-year plan. In business, if you can successfully implement a ten-year strategy, you're considered CEO material. But according to the tacit rule of marriage, when you are in your early twenties, even though you may not be completely formed yourself, you should be able to select a partner who will be equally suitable when you're over 70. What makes things harder is that young people aren't even sure what qualities are required in a long-term partner. The only firsthand experience one has with marriage and how it should be conducted is whatever one has learned at home. But because change is so rapid and so constant in our society, a parents' marriage—even one that remained intact and was relatively happy, itself something of a rarity—may not be helpful as a prototype for future life-styles.

In one study, people who were interviewed said that marriage was "different" from what they had expected. By "different," they undoubtedly meant less romantic. When you're planning for the wedding, you don't anticipate the times when you'll be fighting about whose relatives to visit for Thanksgiving, arguing about who's going to do the dishes, or noticing the strong resemblance your mate bears to a particularly disagreeable parent.

Despite these enormous potential stumbling blocks, we blithely go to the altar promising to live together "happily ever after"—in other words, harmoniously and permanently. "In order to prove love you must disregard every practical consideration in making a marital choice," Mead observed. While it may be true that opposites attract, she suggested that "to have a happy marriage, the mates should be as much alike as possible." Surely she was referring to the holding of similar values, a notion with which most happily married people strongly agree. Yet the people we surveyed had, in prior marriages, routinely taken the vows of marriage after few or no conversations with their partners about long-term goals and how they should be achieved.

Given all the circumstances she described, Mead concluded that it was inevitable that divorce would become commonplace. Once you have an unlimited number of choices in any type of situation, you raise the odds of making a wrong one. And if we philosophically agree with the idea of freedom of choice, then we must also acknowledge that no choice is irrevocable. Being free to choose means being free to choose again. If our freedom to choose any type of marital partner is a reflection of the true American spirit, so too is the prevalence of divorce.

There's an amusing historical precedent for this. In *Divorce: An American Tradition,* author Glenda Riley says that after the United States declared its independence from Britain, people were inspired to write divorce petitions that said, in effect: "My husband is tyrannical. If the U.S. can get rid of King George, I can get rid of him."

Not only did Mead suggest that divorce is inevitable in our culture, she also suggested that it is appropriate—and perhaps even part of the natural order of things. In very simple societies, she pointed out, you learn early in childhood what kind of adult behavior is expected, and then you wait until you grow physically large enough to carry out your destiny. But people in more complex cultures go through a stage of adolescence, "a period of reexamination and possible reorientation of the self toward the expressed goals of society."

Here's the really interesting heart of her theory: "In cultures like ours, there may be a second or a third adolescence, and the most complex, the most sensitive, may die still questing, still capable of change. . . . No one who values civilization and realizes how men have woven the fabric of their lives from their own imaginations as they played over the memory of the past, the experience of the present, and the hope of the future, can count this postponed maturity, this possibility of recurrent adolescent crises and change of life-plan, as anything but gain."

The goal of our society, as Mead pointed out, is mobility and achievement. But when a wife decides that she wants something more out of life and goes to law school, or a husband decides to turn away from corporate life to run a small business, they change not only their occupations but their preoccupations as well. They become quite different people. Even changes that have no immediate dramatic effect— the decision to get in shape or to seek psychological counseling—can, over time, radically alter a person. Developing your strong suits and correcting your weaknesses make you grow. And the person you marry has to grow along with you.

Sometimes, of course, this doesn't happen. "Once there is a recognition that change in rate of growth is simply a function of living in a complex modern world, then the marriage that is developing a dangerous discrepancy may be given professional help," Mead suggested. And if that doesn't solve the problem? Mead said that the discrepancy should be agreed upon as a legitimate but not shameful reason for divorce. "Failures to grow [should be treated] as tragedies but not as personal betrayal. . . . Divorce should not be associated with failure or sin and should not require accusations or collusion, but announced publicly with the same gravity and dignity that went along with announcing the marriage in the first place."

An underlying suggestion is that the more interesting and complex you are, the more likely you are to change. And the more you change, the greater the chance that the partner whom you chose when you were a different person will no longer be the right companion for you.

"A world in which people may reorient their whole lives at forty or fifty is a world in which marriage for life becomes much more difficult," Mead said.

Why divorce is on the rise

In the half-century since Mead's study was published, divorce has become increasingly commonplace. There are several explanations.

Great numbers of women have joined the work force at every level, and in every type of occupation. Since families are smaller, women are occupied for fewer years with child rearing and have more time to pursue careers. This has two implications.

One is that women are less likely to stay in a marriage for economic reasons. Sixty percent of married women with children at home are earning a paycheck. Many women, in fact, outearn their husbands. So, more women have the option to leave a marriage in which they are unhappy. Anthropologist Helen Fisher, in *The First Sex: The Natural Talents of Women and How They Will Change the World,* says we are simply returning to an ancient tradition. According to her, the "divorce rate" was also high among the hunter-gatherers who roamed the earth, scavenging food, before the invention of agriculture left women tending the home while men plowed. The divorce rate is high today for the same reason. "When you have women with careers outside the home who can support themselves and aren't tied to the land, they don't have to remain the subordinate partner in a bad marriage. They can look for a better marriage that's a partnership of equals."

Also, the presence of more women in the workplace creates many new opportunities for social interaction. The more rural and isolated the areas in which they lived when they were housekeepers, the fewer opportunities American women had to socialize. Increasingly, we live in suburban and urban communities, and, what's more, men and women have begun to work together in factories and offices, even precinct houses and construction sites, on a daily basis. Undistracted by the petty details of mundane life; working together, sometimes intensely and for long hours, in pursuit of a common goal; and learning to admire and respect one another's skills and talents in close quarters, men and women may develop an attraction which becomes sexual—whether or not fraternization is sanctioned by the company or an extramarital relationship was initially sought by either party.

We're living much longer. An American born in the 1940s had a projected life-span of only sixty years. Couples who pledged to stay together for a lifetime when Harry Truman was the President weren't making nearly as long a commitment as a couple making similar vows today. Mead wrote about reorienting oneself at age 40 or 50; but today, many, many people remain vital and active for three or four decades after that.

What draws you to a partner in the first place is generally some kind of physical attraction that has to do with reproductive suitability. For example, scientists suggest that both humans and animals are attracted to symmetry because it indicates both good health and healthy genes. As Nancy Etcoff writes in *Survival of the Prettiest,* "What was biologically advantageous became an esthetic preference." So in every culture men are attracted to luxurious hair, delicate jaws, narrow waists, and full hips and lips—all of which indicate youth and a high estrogen level, and thus predict fertility; for their part, women are attracted to men who are tall and muscular, with the broad shoulders and square jaws that testify to a high testosterone level and, by extension, the ability to protect and provide for a family.

But the person who is genetically complementary and a great biological mate may not be the golfing companion or intellectual counterpart who will fit your needs down the road. Except for a relatively brief span of years, what you're looking for in a partner has less to do with his or her gene pool than his or her ability to keep you entertained and interested. Consequently, sexual attraction is less of a factor than it seems to be in your youth. And as you mature, money and power can be as compellingly attractive as someone's physical appearance. As Henry Kissinger famously remarked, power is the ultimate aphrodisiac—though its impact may be less seductive on a woman in her twenties looking for someone to have children with than on a woman in her forties looking for the man who can help her achieve a nice home and security at retirement.

Another reason that you may be tempted to look for a new partner over the course of time is that the urge for novelty is compelling: It is an inborn human trait. Scientists have discovered that both shyness and extroversion are genetically determined characteristics, and one of the components of the latter is an innate preference for different sorts of stimulation. People who are programmed to be extroverts may find it contrary to their nature to stay in a lifelong marriage to one partner.

Another reason that divorce is on the rise is that "Baby Boomers," who were in their infancy while Mead was writing, are a different breed than the generations who preceded them. First, they have generally accepted the idea that they are entitled to personal growth, freedom, and self-fulfillment, and that society is virtually obliged to provide these conditions to everyone. They are far more likely than their predecessors to be willing to attempt profound changes in themselves—through therapy, increased education, and spiritual questing—in the course of their lifetime. And, ultimately, they may be unwilling to honor a commitment (such as marriage) that hinders their quest for personal fulfillment. Second, social and religious codes, if not abandoned altogether, are interpreted far more flexibly. Divorce is not taken to represent a deep breach in the moral code. Furthermore, society has become more tolerant of alternative life-styles such as homosexuality or living the single life. Finally, people in general seem more interested in present gratification than in the prospect of a future life of happiness as the reward for a life of forbearance. There doesn't seem to be any point to, or honor in, staying in a bad marriage.

Helen Fisher, who has surveyed courtship, sex, and pair-bonding from prehistory until the present, says in *Anatomy of Love* that "love is a primitive but elegant emotion, like fear and surprise." She identifies two stages: "The infatuation stage is associated with a natural amphetamine high, caused by a chemical produced by the brain. After that comes the more calm attachment stage—an addictive need for the other person, produced by a morphine-like substance released in the brain." When the first stage wears off, that creates a natural weak point in the relationship. "Rather than recognize this weak point and work through it, we tend to abandon the relationship altogether," she says, which is easy in a society where divorce no longer carries a stigma.

"Over the years," agrees matrimonial attorney Arthur D. Ginsburg, "I have observed that the two major reasons why people get divorced have remained constant. They're just what you might expect. Either the situation at home was completely intolerable (a partner was promiscuous, using a substance, or physically abusive), or the person wanted out because he or she had fallen in love with another person. But in the last couple of decades, I have seen another trend: people have gotten a divorce simply because they aren't satisfied with their lives. It's not that they are acting rashly, particularly where there are small children involved. But if they just aren't happy in their day-to-day lives, and if this can be blamed on the marriage, they're not willing to stay in it."

An increase in the number of divorces is a self-perpetuating trend. If divorce is increasingly seen as an easy option, people may be more willing to consider it.

These modern factors, taken in tandem with those identified by Mead, explain the increase in the divorce rate. What we now may have to do is change our attitude about divorce and, like Mead, come to the conclusion—unusual at the time she was writing and not widely held today—that a divorce should be seen not as a failure but rather as a legitimate and compelling need to change partners. If we recognize the truth in this, we may come to see the end of a particular marriage as an inevitable human passage. Instead of a pairing for life, we may have sequential monogamy. There's certainly plenty of precedent for this; throughout nature, there is a recurrent pattern of endings and beginnings, decomposition and renewal. A remarriage is a kind of rebirth.

Some people have gone so far as to argue that remarriages are the most successful marriages of all.

I've been married three times and although a trifecta wasn't exactly in my life-plan, in a way it worked out for me better than I might have guessed. My first husband, the father of my kids, was organized and nurturing. I was very young when we married, and I was building my career. I know I wouldn't have done nearly as well as I did if he hadn't been so helpful with the kid-raising stuff. He was a lot more involved with the details than I was. He was the point guy with the pediatrician. He negotiated the diaper service. But he earned very little money and he wasn't ambitious, and I was. Over time, we became part of different worlds, and we divorced after twelve years. I remarried a guy who wasn't at all interested in children, but he was very driven. He wanted to make a lot of money. We had a couple of homes and lived very well. He bought jewelry, art, real estate. Best of all, he was willing to help with the kids' huge camp and school expenses, since my first husband couldn't really contribute a lot. The bad news was that he was a workaholic, and after a while he was just too intense, while I was ready to cut back on work and start enjoying life. After ten years, we went our separate ways. And then I married my present husband. He's more laid back, he shares more of my interests than either of the other two [did], and he's the guy for me to retire with.

—Helen, 58, writer

Most people would rather be married than not. Like the people we surveyed, even if marriage isn't in their plans, it probably is in their future. Certainly being half of a couple has practical social advantages. Though the ancient Greeks liked to have an odd number of guests at their dinner parties (they considered even numbers "feminine" and odd numbers "masculine," and the latter were more auspicious), most social events today work on an older model, that of Noah's ark. People are often more welcome when they come in pairs.

In addition, marriage is good for your health. The conventional wisdom was that men in particular lived longer and enjoyed better health when married. An August 8, 1998, story in *The New York Times* reported that scientists had discovered that marriage benefits women as well. The findings indicated that men and women who have suffered an emotional illness have a more extensive recovery, and a higher rate of recovery, when they live in a social network—and being half of a couple usually helps you build a larger network.

But the most compelling reasons people remarry are the same ones that made them marry in the first place: for love, companionship, and sex. The need to have a satisfactory and complete relationship is formalized in the institution of marriage, and however imperfect it may be, a marriage usually provides at least an illusion of comfort and familiarity. In her book *Larry's Party*, novelist Carol Shields says it nicely: "A happy marriage, whether it's long or short, gathers a kind of density around it, the easy verbal slippage of 'my wife,' 'my husband,' and the swing-in-the-garden sense of 'we always'—fill in the blank—'We always take vitamin C when we're coming down with a cold,' 'we always stay home Sunday night,' 'we always cancel the newspaper when we're away for a week.' And the collected hours of joined sleep, they add up to certain assurances about love too: that even if you leave love alone it forms a cocoon around you."

Wanting that comfort, most divorced people choose to remarry if the opportunity presents itself. They also choose to work harder at making the remarriage survive. They go into it knowing full well that there will be problems and moments when, as one woman said, "You'll just have to grit your teeth or put a bag over your head." They know that there will be periods when you will love your spouse very much and other times when you'll wonder what you were thinking when you agreed to marry this person. And they are aware that the bad patches can last for days or even weeks. Knowing all this, they make a commitment—not just to their partner but, more important, to themselves—to stick with it. And many of them succeed.

This book is not simply about remarriage. It is a book about the process of building a relationship and the changes one goes through to move from a broken marriage to a successful one. The first part of the book covers phase one of the process: the journey toward remarriage. Putting closure on the first marriage, rebuilding your self-esteem, and acquiring enough self-knowledge to ensure that you won't repeat the same mistakes are all involved in the first step. Next, you must engage in the process of searching for a new partner. When you think you have found the right one, you need criteria to judge how well you are suited to one another and how well you will fit into one another's lives. We'll help you sort things out.

The second part of the book covers the next part of the process: making the marriage successful. That means anticipating and finding practical ways to deal with the three biggest stumbling blocks: problems with former spouses, children, and money. It also means finding positive ways to support and accommodate one another.

The many voices you hear throughout the text are those of people who have successfully completed this same journey. They will echo and answer many of your own thoughts and concerns.

Despite the pervasiveness of the myth that remarriages are, to paraphrase Santayana, a case of people condemned to repeat the past, the fact is that the majority of the people we surveyed had learned enough from their prior mistakes to avoid making them again. They were, overall, extremely happy. We hope this book inspires you to emulate their successes and find happiness of your own.

Part One

JOURNEY
TO REMARRIAGE

1

PUTTING THE PAST
BEHIND YOU

Many people have told me that divorce was the worst thing that ever happened to them and it was also the best thing that ever happened because of the changes that occurred in them. They ended up so much stronger and wiser.

—Audrey Wentworth, family therapist

It is impossible to exaggerate the amount of trauma and the degree of feelings of failure and loss that are associated with the end of a marriage.

Fred and I got together in college and married immediately after graduation, then packed our few possessions and many books and went off to graduate school. The marriage started to deteriorate very quickly.

Fred totally immersed himself in his studies, and I felt abandoned and isolated. I wasn't looking to get involved with someone else, but shortly after I started my second year of graduate school, I found myself swept up in a passionate affair with Brent, a wildly attractive and charismatic colleague. Within months, I had divorced my husband in order to marry him. One night, in our third year together, he turned to me, said, "I don't feel well," and died. He had had a cerebral hemorrhage caused by a congenital problem. It's twenty years later, and I have a new husband and children, but I can honestly say that going through that early divorce, even though it was at my instigation, was a lot more shocking and unsettling to me than Brent's death. I guess it made me profoundly aware that nothing is forever.

—Caroline, 55, university professor

Adding to the pain of divorce for many people is the feeling of being judged by a collective external conscience that is assigning them blame. But a spouse may also experience feelings of failure and guilt even if the marriage was terminated by death. You may think, If I had done more—pressured my spouse to take better care of himself (or herself), helped with the economic burden to reduce the stress on my spouse, spotted the signs of illness earlier, tried harder to find new doctors—then things might have turned out differently. In addition, you may have other, unresolved issues stemming from the marriage, ranging from anger that the spouse has "left" you to remorse for acts of omission (not having been thoughtful or loving enough) or commission (having resented the need to care for an ill spouse; having been unfaithful). Or you might simply feel guilty for having made such a wrong choice.

A big source of stress for me is my guilt about the failure of my first marriage. Counseling has helped me quite a bit. I'm not sure I will ever fully overcome it, but I don't dwell on it anymore. I can now tell someone without feeling embarrassed that I rushed into my first marriage.

—Ruth, 25, data entry clerk

Society deems it a failure if you end a marriage after eight years because you're supposed to stay with one person for your whole life. But who has that kind of a plan? You have to think of it as a success if you stayed together for eight years. It's not a failure. It just ended. But not everyone can tell herself that.

—Vickie, 40, music teacher

Along with a sense of failure, it is very common to feel a deep sense of loss in the aftermath of a terminated marriage. Wanting to feel connected and attached is a very basic human desire. For a woman, a marriage may even represent her identity and, in certain communities, her position in the community may be totally defined by her marriage.

Feelings of failure and loss alone may be sufficiently overwhelming to make you want to climb into bed and pull up the covers. But in the face of this trauma, you have to figure out a way to cope and deal with the practical matters that need addressing, ranging from those that concern your own well-being to the obligations you may have to others, such as children and business partners. Though it will be little or no consolation to you at the time—and you may even be appalled at the notion—the terrible feelings you experience may eventually help you to make a happier remarriage.

"I don't think there is a person on earth who, no matter how right his or her reasons for leaving the marriage, doesn't regard divorce as a failure," says psychotherapist Jill Muir Sukenick. "Every one of them has a great desire not to reexperience this failure, which is the impetus for learning what you need to learn in order to make a better choice the next time around."

"People who are in a second marriage have learned what they value and what is special about being married. Your willingness to preserve the institution means you don't take it lightly," concurs therapist Judith Siegel. "This is a life lesson, and it may make you more sensitive to a new partner and more willing to compromise, out of respect for the institution of marriage."

What to expect when a marriage ends

WHAT WERE THE CIRCUMSTANCES OF THE DISSOLUTION?

If it was a mutual and relatively amicable decision that you should go your separate ways, you will experience some pain. Your grief of course will be far greater if your spouse died, or if the marriage broke up as the result of serious incompatibility, anger, hostility, betrayal, or abuse.

The negative feelings associated with the breakup may catapult you back to an earlier time in your life, specifically your adolescent years, when you began interacting in new ways with the opposite sex and you probably experienced typical anxieties regarding your popularity—or lack of it. In the wake of a divorce, you may experience the present as the past. Now becomes then. If your spouse announces that he or she is leaving you for another person, this blow to your self-esteem takes you right back to high school, and you may re-experience feeling "unpopular" and insecure.

The marriage wasn't flourishing, so I filed for divorce. My ex became vicious. He started dating immediately and got engaged before we were even divorced. Then I started hearing about how unfaithful he'd been all during the marriage. Everything I had believed was crashing down on me, and it took me a long time to recover.

—Chloe, 50, artist

Everyone who has weathered the painful dissolution of a marriage describes experiences that are in some ways similar, though the length of time it takes to recover will vary from individual to individual. "In general, however, it appears that most people need at least two years and perhaps as long as five to recuperate thoroughly from all the chaos of divorce," says psychotherapist and certified family mediator Roxanne Permesly, "unless the marriage has been very brief."

"Aside from the emotional issues, you have to work through the practical ramifications, including the costly and time-consuming legal aspects and the lingering and possibly life-changing economic consequences such as child support and alimony or reduced circumstances," she says.

It is natural to have many fears, in many areas:

I was worried about being able to support my children, be independent, pay for insurance; and my biggest fear was making sure my children were going to be emotionally okay.

—Donna, 37, computer artist

You can't tackle all those concerns at the same time. Instead, you have to sort them out. Start by focusing on those that are most immediate. Though taking action may be hard, it will be helpful. Any forward step will give you a sense of being in control.

DIFFICULT LIFE-STYLE DECISIONS

Until you have solved some of the pressing problems in the aftermath of your marriage, you won't be free to focus on changing yourself. Some of the main problems to resolve are:

- Where will you live?
- Will you have a large enough divorce settlement to support yourself, or will you have to work?
- If you have to work, do you have any idea what you will do? Do you have sufficient training? If not, what more do you need, and where will you get it?
- Is there enough money to support your children?
- How are you going to work out the details of child rearing?

If you were divorced, and you and your spouse feel too much bitterness to be able to work out these questions, see if your divorce lawyers can help, or seek out a divorce mediator.

GRIEVING

If your marriage ended as the result of a death, you will probably be offered comfort by friends and relatives. Even if the marriage wasn't particularly happy, even if you harbor guilty feelings about whatever you did or didn't do to make the marriage better, becoming a widow or widower is viewed as somehow ennobling. Still, consider joining a bereavement group or seeing a grief counselor.

These groups are a huge help. Everyone else gets sick of hearing about your loss after a month, and these people can talk to you about it for years.

—Hillary, 51, consultant

There are divorce recovery groups too, which help divorced men or women while they are grieving about the end of a marriage. You may be surprised at how emotionally isolated you become when your marriage breaks up. Friends and family members may not recognize the extent of your feelings of loss. If the marriage was an unhappy one, they might find any such feelings of yours especially incomprehensible.

If one spouse left the other, both parties may be suffering from a combination of anger and guilt. The one who left is likely to feel guilty and perhaps even angry, though the anger may just be a way of rationalizing and justifying being "driven" to leave; the one who was left will most likely feel angry and possibly guilty about some real or imagined shortcoming that drove the other person away.

Grieving may be very intense and it may go on for a long time. You have to expect it and recognize that you cannot put closure on your marriage until this period is over.

SELF-DOUBT

As a young adult, you develop a sense of who you are and how you fit into the universe. You come to rely on your ability to judge people and make decisions. But when your marriage ends in divorce, you tend to reexamine all your values, since things haven't worked out as you expected. It's inevitable that you will question your ability to make decisions and to assess people. The more the divorce caught you unawares (if, for example, you discover that your partner has been emotionally involved with another person), the more pain and doubt you will feel.

When I left him, I thought people were going to ask what I did wrong.
—Norma, 46, beauty salon owner

It was miserable enough being told by my husband that he wanted out of the marriage. But what really took the wind out of me was finding out that not only had he been having an affair for years, but also that all along he had been living with her part-time in an apartment he had rented. I felt like a total fool. I wondered what else I was missing. I thought of a story a friend had told me. She had been in therapy with her husband, a recovering alcoholic, when he complained about some event in the past. She had disputed his account. "You're going to have to accept your wife's testimony," the therapist told him, "since yours is unreliable. Back then, you were looking at life through the bottom of a bottle." I felt like that man. I may not have been looking at life through the bottom of a bottle, but was I wearing blinders, and for how long?
—Claudia, 47, jeweler

After coming out of the totally dysfunctional marriage, I had my doubts about whether I was capable of having a normal, loving relationship with any man, because I thought I was damaged goods.
—Dana, 50, artist

Men have similar experiences:

She ran off with a guy twelve years younger than herself. I was depressed, wallowing in self-pity for a few years [before I was able to get over it].

         —Louis, 46, small business owner

FAILURE TO SEPARATE

Some people cling to the past by continuing to have a sexual relationship with an ex-spouse. There's a certain amount of security and comfort in a familiar embrace, and sometimes the sexual attraction lingers long after the relationship has turned very cold.

Stan and I were still very connected physically, even though the one thing we agreed on (practically the only thing we agreed on) was that we absolutely couldn't live with one another. However, because of the kids, we came into contact with each other frequently, and of course he came by at least once a week to pick them up or drop them off. So I thought it was harmless to have sex with him: I didn't have to worry about getting AIDS, and he knew how to turn me on, and I felt a lot less tense having sex than not having sex. But what I realized was that for me, and probably for most women, having a sexual relationship kept me involved with Stan. I couldn't really begin to care for another man while I was continuing to sleep with Stan. So I stopped it. He was badgering me, what's the difference, can't we be civilized about this, but I just couldn't move on while we were still going to bed with one another.

         —Sandy, 43, teacher

FOCUSING ON THE PAST

"Fixed attention equals hypnosis," says Sandra Harmon, relationship counselor. "You have to literally pull yourself out of a situation where you're stuck in dependency and consciously force yourself to get going, to move out of self-pity, which is a tremendously useless and enervating emotion. When self-pity comes in the door, open the window and let it out. Make it your constant goal to pull away from the past and consciously divert your attention to something else: eating a sandwich, watching television, reading a book, taking a walk, going out with friends."

I turned into a complete sap. I stayed home for weeks, obsessing about my ex. I looked at the wedding pictures, I wondered "What if?" and whether we had made a mistake and what we did wrong. Every place I went and everything I did reminded me of how it used to be. I spent months pedaling backwards. I wouldn't keep a single appointment I made. And then one day, I had agreed to do some volunteer work and just didn't show up. A friend of mine called me up and chewed me out for disappointing everyone—the people I was supposed to work with and the kids we were helping. I guess that was the turning point and finally, slowly, I started moving forward. But it was a misery, and I know I was pretty boring to my friends.

—Lois, 43, literary agent

LOSS OF SELF-ESTEEM

Almost every one of the people whom we surveyed mentioned having "low self-esteem" following the dissolution of a prior marriage.

I thought there must be something wrong with me. Otherwise why would my husband want to end the relationship? I took all the blame, even though he was an angry, emotionally abusive person.

—Mona, 40, music director

Low self-esteem may keep you from attempting to go out and rebuild your life, or it may drive you into promiscuous behavior. Both are unproductive, but the second is actually dangerous.

PHYSICAL SYMPTOMS

Losing a friendship, leaving a job, graduating from school . . . the end of any relationship is a shock to your system and likely to produce physical symptoms. But the dissolution of a marriage is one of the greatest shocks of all. If it has been terminated abruptly—when you had thought things were going well but your spouse just walked out, or if your spouse died—your symptoms may be more acute.

Even if the breakup of your marriage was something of a relief after long periods of unhappiness and tension (whether or not they were accompanied by physical symptoms), your body is still likely to react.

Survivors of domestic violence can experience any of the symptoms described by the National Center for Post-Traumatic Stress Disorder such as feeling irritable, on-guard, easily startled, worried or anxious; having difficulty falling or staying asleep; and experiencing severe nightmares and panic attacks. Hives and other skin problems, bursitis, gastrointestinal problems, and other ailments that are normally aggravated by the catchall term "stress" are fairly common. Have yourself thoroughly checked out by a physician and take palliative remedies if needed to help you get through the worst periods.

Making moves toward recovery

START BUILDING AN IDENTITY AS A SINGLE PERSON

If you've come out of a bad marriage, the rush of freedom is exhilarating and terrifying. Like a teenager escaped from the family, or a refugee seeking political asylum, while you're relishing your new independence, a part of you feels a certain longing for the familiar constraints. You're not Mrs. Somebody any more, or the husband of So-and-so.

A year after the divorce, a man who had been a good friend of ours died, and I asked my ex-wife to come with me to the funeral. She asked me why I thought we should go together, and I said, "Because this is an upsetting situation and I thought we would be there for each other." She said to me, "You don't get it. We're not there for each other. If we were there for each other, we'd be married. It's not appropriate to hang on like this." Honestly, I was completely taken aback by what she said, but after I thought it over, I realized she was right. I had to do everything on my own, including paying condolence calls. I wasn't half a couple anymore. I was just me.

—Bill, 47, foreign trader

But who exactly are you? If you were very young when you first married and had not had time to explore your options, it will take you some time to find that out.

If you were always doing something with your partner because it was something he or she wanted, now you should think about what you would like to do. "Would I like to bird watch?" "Would I like to paint my bedroom purple?" You don't have to put someone else first. You can choose exactly what you want. If you have never spent a lot of time as a single person, you have a lot of self-investigation to do, and wonderful opportunities to indulge yourself. If you like films with subtitles, go see them all. If you want to hang around jazz clubs, eat Moroccan food with your hands, and go visit a nudist colony, do it. This may sound silly, but it's how you'll grow. Most of us enjoyed this process when we were young, but often we stop taking risks and exploring new options after our young-adult years are behind us.

To start a process of self-discovery in the aftermath of a broken marriage when you're feeling tentative and insecure may seem frightening or hard. But ultimately, it will give you pleasure. It's your life, and you can design it yourself. You may even find a new self as you do it. This is a necessary process if you have any intentions of having a happy remarriage.

Live your life as though you will always be single. Don't sit around waiting for someone else or you may become bitter and lonely and wallow in self-pity. Live for yourself.

—Eleanor, 65, real estate broker

Your previous marriage might have failed because you found the right person at the wrong time. You have to take responsibility for yourself. If you can be happy by yourself, only then are you ready for a remarriage. If you can be happy reading, or climbing mountains, or doing whatever it is you do, then you can be happy with another person. But if you're not happy with yourself, you can't be happy with the greatest person in the world.

—Burt, 46, engineer

The trick to living a successful life is to be able to define yourself without including other people in the definition—as someone's wife, or someone's mother.

—Vicki, 40, music teacher

MAKE NEW TIES

"Among the issues you will have to resolve for yourself are those connected to the 'community divorce.' How will people in the community deal with you and your partner? Will you be seen as poor and pathetic, or as a threat to other marriages?" says Roxanne Permesly. You may be disappointed when you look to your family and friends for support. While some of them may rally to your side, you may also have to deal with some disapproval. Your intimates may suggest, perhaps subtly, but possibly quite directly, that you have made a bad mistake in leaving a marriage.

My parents went crazy when I told them I was leaving. They didn't want me to get a divorce. My father told me I was embarrassing the family, especially after the big wedding.

—Kyla, 47, journalist

One mother said to her daughter, "I stayed as long as I was in control of the checkbook. If that was good enough for me, it should have been okay for you." If you were the one who was left, on the other hand, other people may make you feel that somehow you were to blame—by not being attentive enough, or supportive enough, and so forth. If you are already feeling like a failure, this can be even more shattering. Friends may also fail to give you the kind of bolstering you hoped for. People often have trouble coping when death or divorce splits up a couple that was part of their social network. A divorce, especially if it came as something of a surprise, may make other couples feel obliged to take a closer look at their own marriage, which may be uncomfortable for them.

There's also some sense that a broken marriage is somehow "catching." It is not unusual for friends to shy away from someone who is going through or has weathered a divorce, just as—however unfairly and ungenerously—they may withdraw from the company of someone who is very ill. A woman may be excluded sometimes because the other women feel threatened when an unattached female wishes to remain a part of their crowd.

Old friends hardly know what to do with you when your marriage breaks up. It was sometimes a struggle just getting girlfriends to meet for lunch. It's very threatening to a whole circle when the circle is broken, and you often painfully lose friends who you thought were true blue. You don't learn your true friends until you get divorced.

—Faye, 45, songwriter

A man who has relied on his wife to arrange the social calendar may find that few invitations are extended his way, either because his wife's friends are deliberately leaving him out or simply because, being in new circumstances, he has faded from their consciousness. If much of your social life consisted of mixing with your spouse's business contacts, that circle may now also be closed to you. No support system is totally reliable.

Much of my social life revolved around our country club. I played tennis there; the kids attended the day camp; my husband and I attended the social functions. When our marriage ended, I was stunned to find that the club had a divorce policy: Only the husband could remain a member—an economic decision, no doubt. I became persona non grata; I was excommunicated. No one came to my defense. I lost not only a husband, but a whole life-style and circle of "friends."

—Gail, 40, housewife

You will have to work at making your own connections as a single person in every area of your life. Keep up with the old friends who are supportive at this time, but don't join a "First Wives Club" or a group like the one in the movie *Jerry Maguire,* whose members meet only to grouse about their ex-husbands. Avoid the kinds of people who had a very unhappy experience in a prior marriage and have grabbed onto a notion that all members of the opposite sex have a tendency to be insulting, rejecting, controlling, incompetent, or whatever. In such groups any misstep on the part of a potential new partner may invite "universalizing"—making a provocative comment that begins with a phrase such as "Women always . . ." or "Men never . . ."

It's very tempting to try to find solace from a group of people who are bashing former spouses, but obsessing is not productive. When you're constantly surrounded by people who are dwelling on bad experiences, it's hard to look on the bright side. People who have generalized their anger at their exes to anger at all the men (or women) in the world aren't good people to hang around with if you're planning to restart your social life.

My friend Katie was a great companion when I felt like complaining about my husband, because she had an ex she hated, too. Our conversations recalled Fran Lebowitz's line that the opposite of talking isn't listening, but waiting. One of us would tell a horror story and the other would wait for a pause and then contribute one of her own. Katie even told horror stories about other people's exes, and she had a whole circle of disgruntled women that welcomed me into it. I finally realized that hanging around with them was a terrible idea: They gave off such neg-

ative vibes that I was sure no man would come within talking distance if I were anywhere with them. His radar would warn him off.

—Susan, 39, graphic artist

Instead, join special interest groups, accept invitations from co-workers, try sports—anything to help you find new friends. At the very least, you'll enjoy a busy social life; and, of course, introductions from friends are the number one way to find a new partner.

It's important to have plenty of friends, to get your support system in order. It was hard to call my old pals because all I did was talk about my divorce. I decided to use the Internet to find new friends and something else to talk about.

—Dana, 50, artist

"What's important is to find some place to feel that you fit in again, that you have your whole identity. You need to get your whole self back so you won't make another bad choice," Roxanne Permesly says.

THROW OUT THE OLD CASSETTES

Go ahead and blow off steam about your ex to your therapist or your mother, but try to spare everyone else the same old stories of how the ex "done you wrong." Although psychologists once told you that giving vent to your pain or anger was an appropriate way to handle them, new research indicates that doing this over and over again may be a mistake, since you are continually opening the old wounds.

It may be tempting to vent your anger against a former spouse when you're on a date—the conversation may naturally turn to your marriage and why you left it—but it's very unattractive.

I would go out on dates with these divorced women and they'd be carrying on nonstop about their ex-spouses, and I would say to them,

"Let me ask you something. Does this guy pay child support the way he's supposed to?" and they'd say yes, and then I'd ask, "Was he ever abusive—did he ever hurt you physically?" and they'd say "Of course not," and I'd say, "Then why are you so angry at him?" and they'd start ranting and raving. Naturally, I started wondering what my ex was saying about me. I wanted to say to them, "You know, you're talking to someone from the same species as the guy you're vilifying." I'd get this impression that on any given night, there were thousands or possibly millions of divorced women spewing out the very same venom. It was the quickest way to turn me off, no matter how appealing the woman was in every other way.

—Bill, 47, foreign trader

UNLOAD YOUR ANGER AND STOP BLAMING

"The emotional work you go through in a divorce starts with grief, goes to acceptance and then to apologies," says Permesly. At some point you have to accept responsibility for your own role in the relationship.

It's easy to pin everything on the other person. But you have to do work on yourself.

—Roberta, 63, secretary

"I come from a family where people don't get divorced," says psychotherapist Joan Soncini. "At first, I felt only bad people got divorced. I think when one marriage fails, you can say 'I made a mistake,' or blame bad luck. But I'm an object-relations therapist. If you examine your 'luck' you will find explanations for the failure and discover it wasn't really luck at all but things you didn't understand or problems you had in significant relationships as a child. At the time of the second divorce, you have to stop kidding yourself. Something is going on you have to understand. You're not healthy enough, or a spouse isn't, or you don't work things out or try hard enough. The emphasis is not on blaming but about exploring and questioning your-self and your psychological health and the relationship so you don't make the same mistake and continue the pattern of tossing out one spouse and getting another with the same issue."

After I got divorced, I was angry. "How could you do this to me, after all I've done for you?" I thought. "I gave you so many things." But we didn't have the connection we started out with; that [had] left. After I got divorced, I had six years to think about what happened in my life. I realize what I did wrong. Instead of blaming her, I started to look at myself and I knew I wanted to get married again. You need to evaluate, to sit down with a piece of paper and ask what happened. Don't make a list for your spouse—make a list for yourself, and ask what you did wrong. If you take the time to be honest, you'll learn.

—Burt, 46, engineer

I have changed my whole life since my divorce, because I feel it failed in part due to me, and the children are the ones who suffer. I wasn't strong enough to stand up to my first husband, and he needed that. I learned to break the pattern, to realize who I am.

—Maggie, 54, lawyer

"Eventually you should make peace with your partner," Permesly observes. "This doesn't mean you have to end up being best friends. But it does mean that you have to treat an ex like just another human being. Most of us are nice to the gas station attendant and the super-market cashier. If you can't be neutral in your relationship with your ex, you bring a core of hostility and unresolved feelings into the new marriage. Your new partner becomes the scapegoat, and you start in with 'You're just like my ex.' You have to get rid of those patterns."

Make positive changes

"At the beginning of every relationship, the role of the crazy person is up for grabs," Nora Ephron once said. You can't make a higher-functioning second marriage without fixing the thing, or things, that caused the problem in the first place. Despite Ephron's wry comment, it's probably closer to the truth to say that a bad relationship usually involves not one but two crazy people who act in complementary ways, even if one of them appears rational.

If one person is controlling, the other may play the victim. If one is too rigid, the other may become irresponsible. The person who is selfish and can't get enough chooses to be with someone who is selfless and can't give enough. The intellectual who hides behind words and ideas pairs up with a reactive type who operates almost purely from feelings. Opposite needs attract.

CONSIDER SEEKING PROFESSIONAL HELP

One therapist told us that she could not recall ever consulting with a newly divorced patient who did not "externalize" the failure of the marriage. Rather than admit to the possibility of having a problem that acts as an obstacle to a satisfying and enduring relationship, people often try to pin the blame on some other person, or an outside circumstance.

A remarriage may be different from a first marriage, but unless you have learned from what went wrong the first time, warns psychologist Ruth Durschlag, the end result will be that you repeat your mistakes. Whether or not the new relationship will succeed isn't simply a matter of finding the right person but of being the right person.

Don't make the same mistake twice! In order to move out of a failed marriage and into a more successful one, you must leave some of the problematic issues behind. "Sigmund Freud's notion of repetition compulsion—the fact that people tend to recreate past experiences—is very much alive and well. Faced with any of the big

D's—disaster, disability, death, and divorce—you must take stock: Why am I failing? Why am I helpless? Why am I broke? What happened in my first marriage, and what can be different this time around?" says Durschlag. Some therapists believe that by age 18, 95 percent of the traits that lead you to choose a mate are in place. If you continue to feel unlovable, you will continue to attract people who make you feel unlovable, until you identify the mistakes you have made and change them.

It's often hard to have a clear perspective on how you might have contributed to the problems within your marriage, in which case a counselor can help. "After all, some people enter into an arranged marriage and do absolutely fine," points out Permesly. "So even if you picked someone who turned out to have problems, there are things you might have done. Even with major issues like drugs, alcohol, or physical abuse, you have to take some responsibility for your own part in the process. But sometimes in a first marriage, you don't have the maturity or experience to understand that." It takes a lot of strength and courage not only to leave a marriage but to look at your part in why it failed.

But the rewards are huge.

I didn't want to be one of those people who says, "Gee, I sure did learn a lot from my first three marriages. Now I'm ready to apply what I've learned." I might run out of people to practice on.

—Burt, 46, engineer

I definitely should have done more work on myself after my first marriage. I know what I want and what I wouldn't put up with now, but that's only through strengthening my own character through therapy, meditation, and sports activities.

—Gwen, 48, school administrator

I recommend picking a new therapist together before you get married. We began with his but then went to a person we both like who can articulate both of our needs. We began eighteen months before we were married, after three and a half years of dating. We started out discussing issues about time and space.

—Betty, 45, casting director

Holli Bodner, Psy.D., a marriage and family counselor in Sarasota, Florida, says that one of the reasons many people move on from a bad prior marriage to a successful remarriage is that in the interim they have sought professional help. "They have entered individual, marital, or group therapy to address issues related either to their experiences in the family in which they grew up or interpersonal marital issues that occurred prior to or during their most recent relationship."

"After a broken marriage, I try to get people away from the concept of failure and help them to figure out who they are," says Audrey Wentworth, family therapist.

If you aren't the person you want to be, you'll be victimized over and over again. That's not someone else's problem: It's yours. As one man said to us, "There are no victims, only volunteers." If someone can hold your deficiencies (or your imagined deficiencies) over your head, you won't join the marriage on an equal footing. And the opposite is also true: Once you have healed yourself, you can expect a lot more out of a relationship.

I'm 45, and have been happily remarried for eight years. Between marriages, I learned new skills, carved out a career that meant more to me than a job, and went for therapy. I sort of majored in therapy. I went for twelve years. I grew so much, and I started to really like myself. My self-esteem grew. I was very independent and happy being alone. When you are happier with yourself, you're happier with your mate.

—Sarah, 45, guidance counselor

I've been in my second marriage seven years, since I was 27. The first husband you try to please all the time. The second marriage, you're taking care of yourself—looking after number one first. Because if you're happy, then everyone else around you is going to be happy. I took care of business first, and then the love came.

— Alice, 36, massage therapist

"Marital relationships are more complicated than ever, because most women are still conflicted about the roles they should play," Bodner says. "Years after women's liberation gave women new opportunities and first challenged conventional thinking, women still run up against (or face in their own being) the problem of pursuing careers while raising kids. In any event, you can't afford not to address unresolved issues that date back to your previous marriage and before."

Learn how to break unhealthy patterns. Most people learn how to correct bad behavior that has clear-cut consequences. They realize that if they spend too much, their partner may become anxious or angry, or that they can't be unfaithful and expect a husband or wife to stay in a committed relationship. But without help, they may not come to have insight into the underlying and more pernicious problem that caused such negative behavior. Without that insight, they may repeat it. A few of the people to whom we spoke seemed to be heading down this path. For example:

I was married to a guy who was a drug addict. He sat around and watched TV all day and I was forced to work. After the marriage broke up, I was determined to find another kind of man. So I was thrilled by Burt, who was very successful and driven. But guess what? Though he makes enough money, he's forcing me to work because enough with him is never enough. I bring in the money, and I have no power, no rights, no freedom. I'm again under the thumb of a domineering, insecure, distant, emotionally abusive man.

— Carla, 45, bank manager

Carla's fight seems to be about money, but the real issue is her lack of self-esteem. She has to learn to evaluate prospective partners not only with respect to how well they can take care of her financially but also in regard to how well they are willing to meet her need to be valued as a human being. It's a different dynamic.

Even if Carla or anyone else who repeats bad patterns can acknowledge that making such choices makes them part of the problem, that won't make things change. It's not even enough to *will* yourself to behave differently. You have to look inside and ask questions to find out what unhealthy needs motivate you and then address them, or you'll keep making the same mistake.

As Bodner explains, "You have to take the standpoint, 'I am not happy, so I will do this,' rather than acting like the victim, saying, 'My ex did this to me,' or 'He doesn't make me happy.' It's your life, and you are in charge of it. You have to have a personal growth experience prior to and maybe even during a remarriage."

Indeed, we discovered that the unhappiest remarried people we interviewed (commonly in relationships with abusive people) had made the same mistake twice. So if your first husband, for instance, was an alcoholic (or even if you suspect he was), go to Al-Anon and learn how not to be a caretaker (a people-pleaser who enables others to repeat their negative behavior).

But while enabler/addict may be the most destructive pattern likely to emerge in a remarriage, there are others that are unhealthy and unsatisfying. If you are getting help, you should be able to recognize a pattern and be wary of any signs that indicate your second marriage will repeat the patterns of the first.

After my first marriage, I went into therapy designed for adult children of alcoholics. My father was alcoholic, and that had a great deal to do with the first partner I chose. In my household, there was shame and embarrassment and an extreme emotional climate: he's in a good mood; he's in a bad mood. You were always walking on eggshells. Living like that for nine years affected me and my self-esteem. I know that when I look back, part of the reason I got married at 19 was to escape my home life. I catapulted myself into marriage—not the best way to launch a relationship.

—Roberta, 53, government secretary

Find out how to value yourself. In the aftermath of a failure like a broken marriage, many people revisit the pain and dwell on their faults. If you fixate on the shortcomings you have heard or felt—I'm too fat to be loved; my penis is too small; I don't make enough money; I'm a lousy housewife and no one will ever love me—you'll believe they're true when you're feeling low. In fact, they might be completely absurd. Look around you and you will find plenty of people who are less than perfect in many of the same ways you feel deficient, yet they have found people to love them. Why shouldn't you?

PUT YOURSELF IN CONTROL

"Am I a victim or am I a warrior?" That's the question Sandra Harmon, the relationship counselor, recommends asking yourself when you want to dispel a belief about yourself that makes you feel diminished. A victim says, Woe is me, I'm a loser, I can't do it. A warrior says, These are my goals and all these things standing in the way are just obstacles that I will overcome because I am going to get to my goals.

I was in Greece, and a group of us were making a day trip to an island, and when we got there it turned out that to get to this island, you had to jump into the water and swim. Me? I'm from Brooklyn. I don't swim very well. But I decided I wasn't going to be a victim. A victim would stay on board all day and feel sorry for herself. So I did it: I jumped in the water, and I swam to that shore, and I never looked back. That was the absolute turning point in my life. When I had to face difficult things

in my life, with kids and facing the rent when I lost a job, I just said,
I'll do it. I will overcome. This belief makes you strong.

—Jackie, 33, hotel concierge

HELP YOURSELF GROW

Take action! It requires courage and determination to grow into
the person you'd like to be. But there are many options that will boost
your self-confidence and help you come into a remarriage as an equal.

Get more education. It's never too late to learn. Going back to school
and earning a degree was an important, empowering step for many
of the people we surveyed. Education is the single most important
investment you can make in yourself.

After my divorce at age 45, I was stunned to find I was not qualified
for any job that would allow me to support myself. Many companies
would not even interview me because I was one year short of qualifying
for an undergraduate degree. It took all the strength and determination
I could muster to reapply as a continuing ed student. There I was, back
among the 18- and 19-year-olds, finishing my last year. The qualifica-
tions had changed and, among other things, I had to take college-level
algebra and geometry. I wasn't really sure it would be possible, but I
did it. I graduated with the Class of 1997. When I walked across that
stage to accept that diploma, it was one of the happiest days of my life.

—Dana, 50, artist

Take a self-improvement course. Learn a language. Take a course in
car repair. Do something practical, or do something fanciful. Whatever you choose will open up a new path for you: a new career possibility, or new friendships.

What really helped me was taking classes about being a woman and
feeling good about yourself and asserting yourself. I was raised to believe

that girls were supposed to have babies; but I realized that wasn't enough. Basically, that first time, my life was over when I got married. By the time I remarried, I felt that I could do something and I had value. I didn't feel that way before my first marriage.

—Lee, 56, housewife

Conquer a fear. Even CEOs of Fortune 500 companies don't like speaking in front of an audience! Join a Toastmasters club and practice public speaking. Try out for a local theater production. Test your wings.

There's a program called The Singing Experience in New York for people who have a secret (or not-so-secret) desire to be a professional singer. The woman who leads it gives a series of four classes to help the students prepare a song, and then you're all featured in a student recital that's held in a cabaret. It was a turning point for me to be able to stand in front of scores of people, have all those eyes on me, and sing. Barbra Streisand has nothing to worry about, but I felt great about being able to get and enjoy all that attention. My self-esteem just went way up after that evening.

—Clara, 54, university administrator

Meet a challenge. If you've ever fancied swinging from a trapeze, then go and do it. Go to an Outward-Bound-like program, learn to ride a horse, ski, parasail. . . . You'll keep fit and meet people with similar interests at the same time.

Several years after my divorce, I signed up for scuba-diving lessons. Getting that certification was probably the most physically challenging thing I ever did. I was so proud of myself. It also opened up a new social circle for me. I regularly go on dive trips with a wonderful group of people.

—Harriet, 53, freelance journalist

DEAL WITH YOUR PHYSICAL SELF

There's nothing like a good divorce to force you to lose weight.

—Donna, 50, management consultant

One man we interviewed said he suspected the marriage was headed for the rocks when his wife started getting serious about losing weight—and he was right. She sued for divorce around the time she reached her weight goal. That was unusual—most people don't pull themselves together prior to the divorce. Changing their appearance is usually part of the recovery process and a great boost to self-esteem.

I didn't fall apart during the marriage, but I hadn't kept myself up. When I got divorced, I lost fifteen pounds, got braces for my teeth, tanned my body, got my nails done, and bleached my hair blond. I did anything possible to my exterior to make it better.

—Darcy, 43, housewife

I didn't consider myself attractive. I married my first husband, frankly, not because I was so interested in him but because I was flattered that someone was so interested in me! Throughout the marriage, I was over-weight. I didn't like to look at myself in the mirror. I'd read those articles in Glamour *and* Mademoiselle *that told you about great sexual tricks and couldn't imagine having the courage to initiate them. The articles that really baffled me, though, were the ones that addressed the "problem" of the guys wanting sex all the time and how to deal with that. I couldn't imagine that could be a problem! Between my lousy self-image and my husband's apparent low level of interest in sex, we didn't have much of a sex life at all. I just woke up one day and thought, Is that all there is? and I initiated proceedings for a divorce. I made a list of what I wanted out of my new life, and right up at the top was to do whatever was necessary to change the way I looked: not just lose weight, but do a total makeover. I was 40 years old, and I was totally transformed. I'm in a new marriage now, and believe me, I've got a few tricks of my own for those women's magazines.*

—Rhoda, 47, corporate public relations

Of course keeping fit isn't only about your physical appearances—if you're operating as a single parent, you're going to need more energy. You've read the articles about how exercise can raise the endorphins in your body and give you a high: If you haven't experienced this, now's the time to try.

I decided I had to start exercising when I realized that my kids were now totally dependent on me. I thought to myself, I have to stay healthy. I can't die.

—Hillary, 51, consultant

If you lack the motivation to begin an exercise regimen, joining a health club and hiring a personal trainer for a few sessions is an excellent way to get started. But it's not the only option. You can swim, take up rollerblading, or sign up for golf or tango lessons.

A group of friends and I started meeting to take exercise walks in the park. It happened kind of spontaneously, but it became addictive. The more we went, the more we wanted to go. It was amazingly regenerative. We'd walk together and we'd talk; we'd support each other emotionally and push each other physically. That was the healthiest thing I ever did for myself.

—Claudia, 47, jeweler

GET SERIOUS ABOUT MAKING MONEY

For a man, your work and your relationship are intermingled in ways you don't understand. When you lose one, the other changes its meaning. I've read that entrepreneurs who quit their jobs and start companies do it to stick it to their ex-wives: They want to shake up her sense of security a little bit.

—Karl, 58, inventor

Despite the narrowing gap in the earning power of men and women, in general men are still accustomed to being a breadwinner, and they don't anguish about whether they can support themselves after the divorce. In fact, even after paying alimony and child support, most men are better off financially when they're single. According to a 1996 study in the *American Sociological Review,* men's standard of living after divorce rose 10 percent, while women's fell 27 percent.

For stay-at-home-wives, the decline may be even steeper, reports Lenore J. Weitzman, author of *The Divorce Revolution: The Unexpected Social and Economic Consequences for Women and Children in America.* The discrepancy between the life-style such women can afford based on their earnings in the marketplace and the life-styles to which they were accustomed based on their husbands' income is even greater. Becoming financially independent is probably the single most important thing that you can do to prevent making a bad remarriage. It will boost your self-esteem and you'll remarry for reasons other than financial security.

To have self-esteem, you must feel valued. When and whether you find the relationship that makes you feel that way is not entirely under your control. You do, however, have a fair amount of control over your career. It is better to base your self-confidence on work that is meaningful to you and/or that earns you success, rather than on looks that can age, or romance that can evanesce.

Being obligated to support children motivates many women to succeed.

Having a child taught me priorities and how to be grounded. Being responsible for someone other than yourself is the ultimate life lesson.

—Haley, 54, headhunter

Sometimes that responsibility goads them into making achievements far beyond their expectations.

My husband overspent and went into bankruptcy, and left us on the pretext that he would establish himself and send for us. I pretty much knew that was it. I was broke and lost the home, a place we had bought with my money. My youngest was only 3. I went into real estate because I thought I could make money. In a relatively short period of time, I became the top realtor in my city and was able to buy my house back from the creditors.

—Bev, 61, nurse

On Christmas Day, my former husband was supposed to return but didn't, and all I had to give my daughter for Christmas dinner was a bowl of ramen noodles with eggs in it along with two gifts. I lay there and cried. I felt her little arms come around my neck and I heard her say, "Mommy, don't cry. You got me and I got you, so we will be okay." So there I was at the end of my first marriage, alone, in a foreign country, raising a child who was adopted. It was a frightening experience. I constantly asked myself if I would be capable of providing for her financially and be independent enough to get myself through the divorce. The answer to both was yes. Along with my independence, I gained back my self-esteem. I vowed never to rely on anyone else again.

—Julie, 43, salesclerk

Even if you can't achieve the standard of living you enjoyed in your prior marriage, being self-supporting is psychologically empowering and will keep you from making a marriage out of desperation.

I knew before I went into my current marriage that I would be able to support myself if I needed to. This is a more successful marriage because there is less pressure on it.

—Gwen, 48, school administrator

Having work you care about also makes you more interesting.

Look to the future

GIVE YOURSELF CREDIT

You've done it! Every step you have taken to haul yourself out of despondency and move forward with your life has done more than strengthen you—it has made you a more appealing person.

I met this woman online, and she told me that she had four kids, that her husband had left when the youngest was only 2, and she had been supporting them with very little help and raising them ever since. My reaction was, This is a woman who is formidable and substantial. I wanted to meet her.

—Bill, 47, foreign trader

ACCENTUATE THE POSITIVE

Don't underestimate the power of positive thinking. Don't dwell on what you did wrong. Focus on your achievements and then put them in your consciousness. Write down your five greatest accomplishments: maybe your children have given you reasons to be proud, you've done well in your career, or you've achieved a physical goal that you've set for yourself. Acknowledge that you have reasons to be proud.

Once I decided that I'd rather be alone than with a jerk, I came to really enjoy me. I started looking for someone who would love me for me, accept me, and support me in whatever I chose to do. And when I met my current husband, I was able to have a healthy relationship.

—Inez, 40, bank teller

CHERISH WHAT YOU LEARNED

Nothing ventured, nothing gained! No matter how badly the marriage turned out, it was a learning experience. At least you took a risk, and that's a positive thing. Most people regret the opportunities they missed altogether more than the ones that turned out badly.

You learned some lessons about what it is like to live with someone and be close to another person. If you didn't learn any good things, at least you learned not to make the same mistake the second time around.

I learned what I needed and not what someone else needed from me. I learned that a mature love was one where your partner needed you because she loved you, not loved you because she needed you.

—Wally, 58, architect

Going through the dissolution of a marriage should have helped you develop some resilience. "One of the reasons second marriages do better is that as a result of the divorce you've had to deal either with rejecting someone or being rejected. Surviving that makes you feel strong," says Roxanne Permesly.

ENJOY YOUR CHANCE TO START ANEW

My first husband and I grew apart because he worked all the time, though he said he was doing it for the children and me. He was a low-maintenance guy, which meant life was easy, but it wasn't very exciting. He wasn't a participant in my life. Eventually, though, I became afraid that I wouldn't ever have any excitement. My new husband is a challenge. Sometimes it can be explosive. I am very happy now. I think this is a lot more work, but it's more fun. I have big highs and big lows now, as opposed to a flat line.

—Marie, 46, personal shopper

Think of the breakup of your marriage as the beginning of a new life, not an ending of an old one. That may be a cliché, but a cliché is simply a truth that is frequently repeated. Even if your current goal is not remarriage, it's time to move on, to get ready for whatever is coming next.

One woman we surveyed said to us, "A man leaves a marriage when he finds another woman. A woman leaves a marriage when she finds herself." Regardless of whether or not you were the one to leave, you now have an opportunity to start fresh.

My husband divorced me. I had four kids, felt insecure, had no money in my own right. The divorce was awful and had a terrible effect on the kids at the time. But ultimately it was the best thing that ever happened.

—Anne, 63, real estate broker

Many women—and men, too—who marry young never have the opportunity to see what life would be like if they could make all their decisions on their own. You may not have chosen to live as a single person, but now that you've been given the chance, see where it takes you.

Being single enabled me to take charge of my life, career, and interests in a very positive way.

—Louise, 60, dietitian

Making every decision on your own can be overwhelming, but it can also be liberating.

I had an incredibly happy first marriage. When I met my husband Stan, I thought I was the luckiest woman on earth. He was dynamic and charismatic. Together we launched a fashion design business, and we seemed to be joined at the hip. Over the years, we even grew to look alike. Someone later described us then as two round people in black outfits. When Stan died suddenly, I was devastated. But I was forced to

run the business alone or go under. Eventually, I grew to develop con-
fidence in my own talent. Formerly, I thought he was the interesting,
talented one; I brought him coffee, I deferred to him. In a way, I was
really his willing love slave. It was so astounding to me to discover who
I was and what I could do. I lost a huge amount of weight, chucked my
black baggy clothes, and became someone I never, ever would have been
if Stan [had] lived. I don't regret the years with him, of course, but
neither do I regret the chance I've had to become my own person.

—Leigh Anne, 39, business owner

"Even more than the first marriage, the divorce itself, because it forces you to confront reality, may be the growing experience," says psychiatrist Scott Permesly. As is often the case, what seems at first glance to be a terrible misfortune can have unexpectedly positive results.

My first wife and I met in Boston, where she was in graduate school in
business and I was working toward my Ph.D. in biology. I was very
much in love with her, and we married and moved to New York so she
could pursue her business ambitions. After two years of marriage, she
told me she was unhappy, had been unfaithful, and was leaving. For
months, I literally cried myself to sleep. Within nine months, I met
another woman and I married her a year later. We had the same goals,
ones my first wife never shared: a quiet, rural, academic life with chil-
dren. My divorce gave me the opportunity to get some perspective on
what I really wanted. I can't believe that I almost settled for a life that
in no way satisfied my real yearnings.

—Ed, 36, scientist

You will know that you have completely healed from a broken marriage when you can look back on the experience and recognize the growth that came out of it. This is the point when you are ready to open yourself to a new and enriching relationship.

2

LOVE IS WHERE YOU FIND IT

Q: What made you think this husband would make you happier than the former one?
A: He's *not* the former one.

—Atlanta woman, 46, married one year

The speaker may have been flippant, but she was speaking the truth.

Though you may think you're choosing your wife or husband for reasons of the heart, what drives your choice is far more concrete. "The factors that lead you to choose a first spouse are 'overdetermined,'" says therapist Jill Muir Sukenick. "The literature supports the fact that there are innate biological and psychodynamic factors that drive your choice."

When a man and woman are drawn to each other, they literally have the "right chemistry." Biological factors, like attractive physical characteristics that are a sign of good health, attract men and women for reproductive reasons. But it has been suggested that couples are truly "meant for each other" in an even more specific and complicated fashion than scientists currently understand. Remember that "stranger across a crowded room"? One anthropologist goes so far as to claim that a man and woman who have never met can hone in on each other almost as if directed by radar, even when they are in a roomful of people.

Among the psychodynamic factors that bring couples together is an underlying and healthy narcissism that will cause you to gravitate toward someone who looks like you, someone you might like to resemble, or someone who may be able to compensate for your deficits. "There are many fantasies in a first marriage," says Sukenick. "You may have a fantasy that someone will become a multimillionaire and take you away from your dreary existence. You may fantasize that you will make someone over or find or define yourself through that person. That person will rescue you, make your life better, fill in the gaps you see in yourself."

While the initial attraction may have been biologically and psychologically determined, the decision to actually set the date, book the church, and hire the caterers may be quite capricious, including but obviously not limited to such reasons as: "Everyone else in my sorority is getting married" "I can't stand my family and this looks like an easy out"; and, "Oh my god, I'm pregnant."

A rash, desperate, or thoughtless act made by a very young person is how almost all of the men and women we surveyed described their decision to marry the first time.

They married to please others.

I was just 20. I married the person my parents thought I should marry.
—Kyla, 47, journalist

My mom hadn't been well and she so wanted me to be settled with a family of my own before she had to leave us behind.

—Faye, 45, songwriter

I wasn't looking for anything in a marriage. I was a junior in college and my girlfriend got pregnant, and I married her—what was called "the right thing" at the time.

—Frank, 59, real estate agent

Others did it to escape from home.

I was very young, from an alcoholic family. I think that I just married that first time to get away from that situation.

——Wanda, 42, business owner

He thought I was pretty, we had a good time going to parties, and I was looking for a way to move out of my parents' house.

—Ivy, 28, housewife

They did it to acquire an identity.

I was 18, and I thought he was my ticket to maturity. I'd be a Mrs. Someone, and a grown-up. He wanted me to be the pretty young thing, mother of his kids, someone with no power.

—Lynda, 54, therapist

Or they married as an act of defiance.

I think I married him because my mother always said, "You never finish anything you start," and I wanted to prove her wrong.

—Cyndi, 45, artist

They did it because they thought they'd be "rescued."

I was looking for someone to save me.

—Donna, 50, management consultant

Or they married for lack of another option.

I wasn't interested in getting married, but my family pushed it. My stepmother said, "If you don't think you love him, did it occur to you that you are not lovable?" He was nice, but I wasn't ready. Still, rather than disappoint everyone, the good girl in me married him.

—Bev, 61, nurse

Some seemed to do it so they'd never again have to worry about getting a date for New Year's Eve.

When I married my first wife, more than anything I just married out of the fear of loneliness.

—Ray, 55, abuse counselor

I was 23, and I remember thinking, If I don't marry this person, maybe no one will ever love me that much again.

—Hank, 53, photographer

And some did it the way salmon swim upstream: blindly and for no reason they could explain.

Our relationship was based on the fact we had a good time.

—Darcy, 43, housewife

You were supposed to get married and live happily ever after. It didn't matter who you married. He was just someone I saw on Saturday nights, and then I married him.

—Debbie, 58, social worker

I hadn't seen any action for a year and a half because I was trying to make the top third of my class at Harvard (which I did). I then went to Cape Cod and this girl came by, swinging her hips and signaling, "I want you." We got married thirteen days later and the marriage lasted three months.

—Bob, 61, investor

I married the first girl who would sleep with me.

—Louis, 46, small business owner

It was time to get married. I don't think I thought about it very much. In fact, I know I didn't think about it very much.

—Maggie, 54, lawyer

Although none of these individuals seem to have understood what they were getting into, a few were sophisticated enough to realize that they were making a big mistake—though they went through with the ceremony anyway.

My previous marriage was the result of a near-death accident and my growing sense of mortality. Although even at the time I knew I was entering into that marriage for all the wrong reasons, I felt compelled to secure some sort of a future for myself. I honestly talked myself into the concept and the viability of that marriage. I consider myself to be a bright, intelligent woman, but the thought of spending the rest of my life unattached was more than I could bear. Looking back, it seems so sad that I would take what should be considered a sacred vow and belittle it by "settling."

—June, 37, doctor

Walking down the aisle, I knew it was wrong because I was used to a higher standard of living than he would ever aspire to.

—Helen, 58, writer

I knew I was making a major mistake on the day of my wedding, but I couldn't figure out how to get out of it because it was being held at The Plaza Hotel, which was a very big deal.

—Kyla, 47, journalist

I knew I shouldn't be getting married, but I didn't want to hurt anyone's feelings. I went in knowing I'd go out. I had a big wedding at an estate. There's not one picture of me smiling.

—Haley, 54, headhunter

I knew it was wrong from the beginning. I got pregnant right away so I didn't have to return all the gifts.

—Debbie, 58, social worker

Another chance to get it right

"One reason second marriages do better is the very fact that they are not based on the same kind of dumb decisions as the first one," says psychotherapist Roxanne Permesly. When you're looking for a re-marriage partner, you're older. Having weathered one marital experience, you are probably wiser. By now, you may have learned to distinguish between falling in love with someone and choosing a partner for a lifetime. You may know "love is forever" and "love conquers all" are simply notions—enduring and triumphant love requires work.

In looking for a remarriage partner, you're less likely to search for a fantasy. One remarried spouse said it well.

This marriage works because I have grown up a great deal. I am willing to work harder at things and relationships. I have accepted the fact that everyone has shortcomings. Part of that is from maturity. Part is from experience.

—Jackie, 35, teacher

Chances are you'll go into marriage with your eyes open the second time—less likely to be "blinded by love" or influenced by stereotypes. As a result, you'll look beyond the obvious to qualities that are more significant than "He's attractive," or "She's sexy." Sukenick suggests that "If people make better choices the second time around, it is because the balance of forces that are driving them has changed somehow. They may have gone through therapy, done some soul-searching or had a life experience that increased their awareness and influenced their choices. They are judging others by standards that are good indicators for the potential success of the relationship. The choice may be determined less by instinct and more by logic." Certainly that's what the people we interviewed indicate.

I fell head over heels in love the first time around. I only cared that I loved the man and didn't look to the future. But when I made a re-marriage, I chose a man who was my best friend.

—Annette, 48, health care professional

When I got married the first time I was only 19 and didn't have a clue about what marriage involved. He was 27 and didn't know either. Now, twenty years later, as I prepare for my second marriage, I know who I am, what I want for the rest of my life, and what kind of man I want to spend the rest of my life with. We learn from life's experiences, and if you hold out for what you are really looking for, you will probably not be disappointed.

—Miriam, 45, speech pathologist

If you've learned anything at all, you've learned to scrutinize your choice a lot more carefully.

When you're young, you pick your partner with a searchlight. You run that light over a sea of women, and if you pick up a glint, you say, "Yes, that looks good." In the second marriage, you're using a flashlight. The beam is narrower and more intense. You're looking at the person much more closely.

—Bob, 61, investor

Keep your options open

"The man that I marry. . . ." "The girl that I marry. . . ."

When we conjure up an ideal spouse, our wish list may be very long and may even include qualities that are mutually incompatible. A woman may want a man who is in touch with his feminine side but who is also a fearless, take-charge kind of person, a man who will get mushy at sentimental movies but be a steel-jawed pillar of strength at other times—your basic Clark Kent/Superman combination. A man may want the Madonna of the Vatican and the Madonna of MTV rolled into one. But actual human beings with those kinds of contradictions don't exist.

Usually, men are not very specific about the sort of woman they are looking for. Their advertisements in magazine or newspaper personals make this clear. They may mention particular physical attributes ("slender," "blond"), but otherwise, with one exception, men tend to use very general terms to describe their ideal partner ("loving," "romantic," "pretty," "athletic," "attractive," "fun-loving"). Men are specific in what they're searching for if the previous marriage ended in divorce, says one professional matchmaker, in which case they consciously seek a woman who is very unlike the former spouse.

I made a list of my criteria. I asked for a woman who was tall, thin, blond, had her own money, was really good-looking, wanted sex a lot, and was at least fifteen years younger than me because I had had a bad experience with a woman who was four years older. I would go over

the list to myself in the shower: "I want to meet a woman who is. . . ."
I got exactly what I asked for, though it didn't dawn on me on the first
date that she was the one.

—Louis, 46, small business owner

Women are less likely to stay away from a particular type just because the first model in the series didn't pan out, and, unlike men, they are quite specific about the kind of person they want. They are very organized about their goals and particular about the qualifications they seek. Women who place a personal ad often list many details: "well-dressed, fit, driven, with edge and artistic bent"; "very social, enjoys tennis, exotic travel, and skiing"; "educated, thoughtful"; "intelligent, upscale, handsome GQ-type professional, financially secure, stable."

But you can't choose a mate like you do a car, picking a specific model and then adding on optional features. Many people are surprised to find that the person to whom they are happily remarried doesn't fit the profile of the person they had been originally looking for. Perhaps that's because the image they conjure up is defined primarily by appearance and items on a personality resume, whereas in real life it is a total person whom they find engaging.

I am very tall, and I couldn't stand dating a shorter man. In fact, I
always was attracted to men who had a certain look. My first husband
fit the specs exactly: tall; lanky; dark; rugged features. He had everything
I was looking for, and also something I wasn't—a girlfriend on the side.
When I found out he was having an affair, we got divorced, and I just
immediately started looking for his replacement: tall, lanky, etc. I went
to a New Year's Eve party and started talking to a short, fair, round
guy about basketball, about which we were both passionate. We even
made a bet about a particular statistic and agreed that the loser had to

cook dinner. When I won, he graciously prepared an incredible meal. Over time we just developed a great friendship, and I never took it seriously because—get real!—he was so *not my type. But guess what? I fell in love.*

—Bonnie, 30, paralegal

My friend and I were having lunch. She told me she'd met the most wonderful man and just wished she knew someone to introduce him to. I almost choked on my salad, then asked if she had considered me. She said she had thought I wouldn't be interested. It seems my friends thought I'd date only Tom Selleck types. It's true I did have a mental image of my ideal man. "Tell me about him," I said. "Is he tall? I love tall men." "No," she said. "He's only about five-foot six." "Well, does he have a good physique? Does he work out?" I asked. She wrinkled her nose. "Well . . . he sort of has a tummy." "Does he have hair, then? I haven't been out with a man with a full head of hair for fifteen years." "He's creative," she said. I groaned a little inwardly. "Okay. How about his teeth? I have a thing about teeth. Does he have perfect teeth?" I saw the look on her face.

"Give him my number," I said anyway. I have always been adventuresome and willing to go on blind dates—even with someone who was clearly wrong for me. He called and we talked for two hours. One night later he came to pick me up for dinner. I opened the door expecting Quasimodo; instead, a cherub bearing flowers and smiling from ear to ear was at the door. He turned out to be the most incredible man I've ever met in my life. And yet the first time we went out to dinner, the earth did not move. He was just a nice man. We went out a second time, and then a third. On the third date, I mentioned that my dream was to visit Australia. He invited me to go there with him. I said that we hardly knew each other, but a little later I might consider it. In the first year, we went on eleven trips. He was fun and easy to get along with, and we decided to get married.

—Anne, 63, real estate broker

I thought he looked grubby, and I didn't like that. I was a little snobby. It turned out that he was a very successful businessman who happened to have been working on his boat that day.

—Bev, 61, nurse

We really liked each other back in high school and were good friends, but we only held hands and kissed, and I wound up with someone else. I called him up before our twentieth high-school reunion and convinced him to come. We got together and the sparks were still there. He is balding on top. He was twenty pounds overweight. But as far as I was concerned, the only thing different was that we were both mature.

—Cyndi, 45, artist

I hate when women say, "There are no men around." If you're going to look for hard bodies and the outside, you deserve what you get. Be open to everybody. It doesn't matter if he's six inches shorter, six inches wider, from a different educational background, or in a professional job. Just keep yourself open for someone who makes your heart sing.

—Anne, 63, real estate broker

It became clear in our interviews that many people with happy remarriages were not immediately smitten by the person whose qualities ultimately won them over.

I had always thought that I should be with a man in the mold of my father and my first husband: strong, masculine businessmen, who didn't talk much except to exert their authority and boss people around. I'm not sure why this appealed to me, because I wasn't a bit like my mother, who turned herself into a pretzel for my dad. I was what my father and husband called "opinionated," which was their shorthand for, "When Shakespeare wrote The Taming of the Shrew, *he might have had you in mind." After my marriage ended, I explored a lot of new possibilities for keeping myself busy, and I wound up fundraising for the local community theater. Its artistic director was, in every way, the opposite of my father and husband. He was a terrible businessman, but a caring, intelligent person who was thrilled to have me take charge. So I married him.*

—Veronica, 37, caterer

I met him in the building I moved into after my divorce. He was the ex-roommate of my neighbor's husband, and he came to visit them a lot. He was good and kind and smart and nonthreatening. I went out on dates, and he'd baby-sit for my children. He wasn't someone I thought of as a husband.

—Barbara, 46, personnel specialist

Let people in. People would say, "He's bald," or, "He's twelve years older; that's too old." Really, these things don't matter. The age difference? You can marry a man your own age and he can die. If someone's good to you and fun, give it a chance.

—Lauren, 55, human resources director

The most important thing I would say to someone considering remarriage is to be more open to differences. At first, I was scared about dating my husband. I didn't think he was my type. I see young people go out with someone once or twice and then write him off. If someone tells you, "I was arrested forty-two times," or, "I like to have sex while chained to a cement wall," okay, don't see him. But don't establish all the characteristics in advance. Spend time with different people, listen to them, talk to them. You may find there are surprises.

—Hillary, 51, consultant

Look below the surface

One of the most important things you are looking for is someone with integrity. "How does this person treat you, your children, and his (or her) friends?" asks therapist Roxanne Permesly.

A big factor is that my husband gets along with everyone in my family—my kids, my parents, my siblings. I didn't have that with my ex, and it's a big relief.

—Dana, 50, artist

"Can you see evidence that this is a person who has integrity, acts maturely, knows how to keep a commitment? Does the person have a positive attitude and find ways to solve problems rather than complain about them? This is what you should be thinking about," says Permesly.

I changed my priorities. I wanted a man who was comfortable within himself, a man who was trustworthy, who didn't mind if I went to church—who would go with me. In the past, this man would not have fit my criteria as far as what a man would look like, where my dreams would go.

—Esther, 49, singer

Sometimes a little gesture says a lot:

I was hurt when my [first] husband left me. I didn't want to go out in public and be "poor Norma." But I didn't want not to be "poor Norma," either. I was on the beach with my children when [my second husband and I] met. I wasn't interested in him myself—in fact I was slightly hostile toward him—but I couldn't get over how much my kids liked him. Finally, we got together. It wasn't really a date. I drove to meet him so he wouldn't have to pick me up at my house. We went out to dinner, and then we walked on the beach. The whole time on the beach, he was carrying a white towel. I was wondering what that towel was for. It seemed a little odd, but I didn't say anything because I didn't want to get personal. I thought maybe he meant to put it around his neck if he sweated, or maybe he was a jock and always carried a towel, or maybe he planned to swim. After we had finished our walk, and before we returned to the car, we went to an area where you rinse your feet before you put your shoes back on. He knelt down and washed my feet, and he dried them with the towel. He had had the forethought to bring the towel. So I decided to give him a chance. We've been married a year now.

—Norma, 46, beauty salon owner

Express your needs

When you are young and inexperienced, as is likely in an early marriage, you may not be fully aware of what will make you happy. One positive result of a failed marriage is that your disappointments may have taught you what qualities you are unwilling to live without. Do you need more intimacy? More consideration? More interests in common?

A bad marriage also teaches you the consequences of denying or ignoring your needs or not making them known to your spouse. Many marriages fail through a lack of communication, without which there can be no real relationship.

Don't rush things

Many people don't wait until a marriage is behind them to choose their new partner. First, they meet someone whom they believe to be a better choice than their present spouse, and then they (or the betrayed spouse) bring the marriage to an end.

I thought I would marry the man I left my husband for. He was the catalyst in my marriage breaking up. We were together for three and a half years but, as time went on, I knew I wouldn't marry him.

—Roberta, 53, government secretary

According to some estimates, in nearly half the divorces in this country, a third person is waiting on the sidelines to be the new partner. This is more likely to be the case for men than for women, doubtless because men in general have more opportunities and more financial freedom. But it can happen with women as well.

I knew I had to leave my marriage. I was so incredibly lonely. I was living in a foreign country. Whatever roots I had made were very shallow. I didn't have anyone who really understood me: There was a language barrier and a social barrier. But the biggest problem was that I had made an inappropriate marriage to a man with whom I had nothing in common. I didn't have any resources, and I was concerned about how I would deal with the children. Then I started an affair with a businessman who came to visit from time to time. I was mad about him for a while, and for crazy reasons of his own, he agreed to take us all on. As fast as you can say sayonara, *I had everyone packed and on the plane, and next thing you know we were living in the suburbs of Manhattan with this . . . stranger. It was a disaster. I hadn't really looked at him as anything more than a ticket home.*

—Julie, 43, salesclerk

Many extramarital affairs don't have what it takes to make a long-term relationship. For one thing, when you are having an affair, your emotions are artificially heightened. The guilt and anxiety connected with an illicit relationship tend to make the relationship seem especially thrilling. (Think of Romeo and Juliet.) When the subterfuge is gone, often the excitement goes out of the relationship. Besides, you tend to invest your partner in an affair with qualities that make your spouse seem very inadequate in comparison. This, of course, is a way to justify being unfaithful. If you can convince yourself that you cheated because of your spouse's flaws, you won't feel as guilty.

Finally, it's easy to romanticize an affair because it's so removed from the petty annoyances of daily life, such as dealing with a teenager's behavior issues, figuring out where you're going to get the money to repair a leaky roof, or grappling with other mundane concerns which can run the gamut from boring to downright depressing. Who wouldn't prefer sneaking off for an afternoon of romance?

Though an affair may provide the impetus to leave a marriage, it usually doesn't result in a remarriage. And when it does, the prospects aren't good. Although in the course of our interviews we saw many successful remarriages that grew out of affairs, we also know that many such remarriages fail, so we asked divorce attorney Arthur D. Ginsburg for his observations on this tendency.

"Many of the marriages that don't work out are entered into quickly, sort of on the rebound," Ginsburg says. If you have been involved in an unhappy marriage for a while, your self-esteem has likely been damaged. It is tempting to turn to either a love affair or a new marriage to restore your confidence. "What happens is that if you've been treated badly by a spouse, any relationship that says, 'You're nice,' looks good to you. People who don't feel good about themselves are likely to mistake their response to 'You're nice' for love."

Although you may not realize it, you're making the marriage only to make yourself feel better, or because you're afraid to be alone. Or you're looking for a mother or a father, and have cast your new partner in the role of rescuer. Neediness clouds your judgment.

After the first marriage, I waited just two months before I linked up with the man who became my second husband. Someone said we grasped for salvation. He was also 20, and his wife had left him for someone else and abandoned the two babies. Neither of us had mourned the losses of our first spouses. We weren't ready to connect to someone else. We didn't have the ingredients to stick together.

—Lynda, 54, therapist

If you marry someone whom you're using just to fill an emotional void or take the place of your pain, you may find some relief for your problems, but you won't have found the cure. That's like looking for a bandage when you have a major, long-term illness. In all likelihood, it's just a matter of time before you cast that person aside—or that person gets wise and drops you.

I was divorced in 1976. I had been a virgin when I got married, and all of a sudden, I was in a world where everyone was sleeping with everyone. I met a woman right away. We had little in common except the sexual relationship. We got married about a year later, and four years later we were divorced.

—Wally, 58, architect

"I would suggest a very long engagement," Ginsburg cautions. "And look at the second marriage with a little more perspective. Don't just deal with your emotions."

Dating people is like having a learner's permit for marriage. Once you've been married and down that road before, you realize you probably need more training. How can you really prepare yourself for something you don't necessarily understand?

—Burt, 46, engineer

As Roxanne Permesly points out, "Picking out a date is not picking out a husband." The happily remarried people we interviewed generally had a long courtship before they decided to take another chance. They advised moving very slowly before making the decision to remarry.

He was only the second person I dated. I don't regret marrying him, but I think when you get out of a marriage, you should spend some time meeting more people. We broke up a few times and had a difficult courtship. I think it would have been better had I dated a little more and been more relaxed.

—Lauren, 55, human resources director

Upon meeting my current husband, I took more time to discover what I was feeling each step of the way.

—Rebecca, 36, sales

Be realistic about your expectations

A partner in a first marriage is often young and still hasn't developed into the person he or she will be. But your partner in a remarriage is usually older and therefore less flexible. The advantage of a marriage between two very young people is that they can grow to be like one another. The flip side of that is that they can grow to be very unlike one another.

When you choose your remarriage partner, you're much more sure of the kind of person you are getting. Make sure that what you see is what you want.

When our best man toasted me and my new husband at what was the third wedding for both of us, he said, "You are not marrying for the promise: You are marrying for what is."

—Harriet, 53, freelance journalist

If you are a man who is dating a high-powered executive, do not assume that she will be willing to turn into a stay-at-home mom after marriage. If you are attracted to a journalist whose dream it is to publish a novel, it's only reasonable to assume that this person will be more interested in pursuing his artistic dreams than in amassing money in pursuit of materialistic goals. It doesn't make any sense to pursue relationships like these unless you are willing to adjust your own goals.

Don't be seduced into a relationship with someone who seems to be a "fixer-upper." Attempts at renovating people usually fail.

Getting into marriage mode

Not everyone makes a conscious decision to start looking for a re-marriage partner. In fact, a great many of the people we interviewed weren't eager to date again. Most of them didn't plan to remarry after their first marriage ended.

I wanted nothing to do with men. I was miserable.

—Lee, 56, housewife

I had decided I was going to give up on [relationships]. I was long out of that. I had my hi-fi system and a good book. One of my colleagues came into the office and said she had a wonderful woman she'd like me to meet, and I said, "Thanks anyway, but I don't go on blind dates or any other kind of dates anymore."

—Jack, 65, lawyer

It didn't even occur to me to remarry. Because marriage wasn't some-thing I ever thought about, even before the first one. I never had mar-riage fantasies or picket-fence fantasies.

—Haley, 54, headhunter

No way. I was anti-marriage. I was disillusioned. I was of the opinion that marriage contracts should be renewed every two years.

—Debbie, 58, social worker

Not at all. I had stopped dating because I was tired of game-playing and I thought women were dating me for my money. I had kids, and a good business, and I didn't need any complications.

—Wally, 58, architect

Never. My first husband was verbally abusive and it was a terrible relationship. Even with four kids, I determined to make it on my own.
—Sami, 68, stand-up comedienne

No. I thought I was invulnerable to falling in love again.
—Arthur, 79, executive

Never. I was single for twenty-four years.
—Esther, 49, singer

No. I thought I would never find anyone I would be as happy with and, besides, being widowed is ennobling. I felt that was meant to be, that I'd be alone, and stronger.
—Hillary, 51, consultant

No way. I was the leader of the boys. I was married for eight years. I left because I didn't want to be married. I had no desire to be married, to be pinned down. I didn't believe in marriage other than to have kids. I told the women I dated that I wasn't interested in marriage. Some believed me but most didn't. They thought I was going to change.
—Peter, 55, artist

Surprisingly, every single one of these people went on to have an extremely happy remarriage. Despite their initial conviction that they would not or could not marry again, each of them eventually made themselves available to meet someone new.

If you yourself have decided that remarriage is your goal and that finding a mate is your task, chances are that you will be successful, in the same way that you are able to accomplish most of the other things you set out to do: get a new job, find an apartment, clean a closet. Getting remarried is very possible: Millions do it every year. It requires willingness to make yourself available for a new marriage and the clarity of purpose to back off quickly if you suspect you're with the wrong person.

If, indeed, you are determined to marry, then there are certain things you should do to help make it happen.

DRESS THE PART

"If you go on a job interview, you don't think twice about dressing to appear professional and competent. Even though what you're really selling is your ability, experience and intelligence, you don't show up in sneakers and sweat pants. Similarly, if women are going out to meet men, they should understand that they have to dress and act in a way that signals what they're trying to put across, which in this case is that they are available for a relationship," says Sandra Harmon, the relationship counselor. "A woman who wants to meet men will certainly be more successful if she is in good shape, dresses in a feminine way, fixes her hair and makeup, goes where the men are—and is approachable and warm. That's how you get their attention."

Of course, it's important for a man to be well groomed, and obviously being fit and healthy-looking is a plus. But since men are biologically programmed to put a higher priority on looks than women do, women have to make some extra effort in this area. It may not be fashionable to acknowledge this, but nonetheless it seems to be so.

I didn't want to be seen as a sex object. I worked hard to get where I was—head of a large division of a big corporation—and I wanted a man who could see me as a person and value me for my soul. But then a friend of mine who has always been very successful finding men said to me that men have to be attracted to your physical magnetism before they get interested in your soul. So I let her do a makeover, help me shop for some new clothes, do the makeup and hair. I felt kind of silly and even a little vulnerable, but the first week I changed my appearance, my neighbor, a very available divorcé who had previously been pleasant but distant, asked me to dinner.

—Susan, 39, graphic artist

"A man doesn't look at a woman and say, 'I want her to be the mother of my children.' His response is a lot less subtle than that. If you flirt and look his way and give him a smile, you're telling him you're approachable," Harmon says. "Chances are you won't attract men wearing a boxy suit. You don't have to be in a leopard-skin bikini, either. Somewhere between the boxy suit and the leopard bikini is femininity."

USE YOUR NETWORKS

Thirty-seven percent of the remarried men we surveyed, and 31 percent of the women, met their partners through friends. Don't be shy about asking friends to help you meet people, and when an opportunity comes up, don't pass it by. Often a friend may see an opportunity in a person that we ourselves might have overlooked.

I was single for eight years and always thought I would remarry. I always seemed to choose the unavailable men: hyper, driven, type-A personalities—men who were totally into their careers. I actually considered one man who had five children from his prior marriage, and, as if that wasn't bad enough, hadn't emotionally detached from his ex-wife. One day, my boss called and said she had someone she wanted me to meet. Though I was absolutely uninterested based on her description, she insisted that I follow through. When I met him, I found that, yes, he was completely unlike anyone I had ever dated before. And that turned out to be a good thing. My boss was objective enough to see what I could not: that I needed a type of man whom I had never even considered. There are two morals to this story. One, it doesn't hurt to have your friends prospecting for you at all times, and two, sometimes they know you better than you know yourself.

—Kate, 51, actress

FOLLOW YOUR INTERESTS

A discriminating person who is interested in buying a top-quality dress or piece of jewelry will probably go to a boutique that specializes in that sort of item rather than head to a department store. You may use this approach when looking for a spouse. If you have a particular type of person in mind, rather than going to a "department store"—a singles mixer where you're just part of a huge, undifferentiated crowd—you may prefer to look in places where that kind of person may be found: a squash court, tennis camp, or film course.

Your mother may have passed along vintage advice that is easily dismissed as corny, but in fact makes sense: If you want to meet a doctor, hang out at the hospital coffee shop. If you go to Las Vegas, you're in the right place to find the playboys. If you are interested in connecting with someone who enjoys his children, check out a law or architectural journal to scout for any conventions being held at Disneyland. And then go.

I used to make a point of taking my kids to kid-friendly restaurants on Sunday nights. Divorced dads would be there having a meal with their children before bringing them back to Mom. The kids would talk to other kids, and the parents would sometimes get to know each other.

—Pat, 42, makeup artist

Although that kind of needle-in-the-haystack approach occasionally pays off, it's a better bet to follow your own interests in the hope that you will meet people who are similarly inclined. One of our respondents found his wife in a cooking course in Tuscany. Another found her husband in a mechanical engineering class. And a third met her match at a tango class. One older woman found her most compatible spouse when she was paired with him at her bridge club. A Texan hooked up with his future wife when he volunteered to work on a committee for the rodeo.

Overall, 11 percent of women and 10 percent of men we surveyed found the people they remarried while pursuing a new sport or interest. And some met their spouse through the new friends they acquired via these activities.

Our survey participants found many other creative ways of meeting people.

Join a parents' group.

On the day that my divorce was final, I finally got up the courage to join the national organization, Parents Without Partners. It's a wonderful group meant to help us and our children cope with our common circumstances. It sponsors family outings, picnics, and discussions, arranges for discounted tickets to events, and so on, and I thought it would be a nice way to socialize with other parents (both men and women) and bring the kids along, too. Our group also holds weekly dances at halls and big ballrooms, which is so much nicer than going to a bar. My current husband was the vice-president of membership, and I was able to see how he interacted with his children while in a group. Fourteen months later, we got married.

—Donna, 37, computer artist

Look around at work. Twenty-five years ago, most of the women in the workplace were in support jobs: they were either secretaries or clerks. Today, male and female coworkers meet as equals, spend days together, and travel as a business team. In the group we surveyed, many remarried men (25 percent) and women (26 percent) met their spouses on the job.

The workplace, if you think about it, is like a petri dish in which you can grow a relationship. There's a combination of propinquity and lon-

gevity, and common thoughts and interests, all working to bring you together. Many husbands are tied up in their work, and their wives have no understanding of or interest in something that matters deeply to those men. It's easy to become attracted to someone who shares all of your interests and enthusiasms, especially when you're with them all the time.

—Dan, 42, accountant

Bleak as their prospects may initially appear, women who are divorced from wealthy men and who have never worked find new doors opening for them. An article in *The New York Times* (June 27, 1999) described "the classic employment route of upper-class former wives—both divorced and widowed—in their 40's and 50's. Reared to expect husbands to be their providers, they are without careers of their own, and usually with a financial settlement too meager to maintain the life they are accustomed to.

"But many can turn to careers in glossy fields for which their particular credentials—high-maintenance tastes and a network of rich and social friends—make them ideally suited. These include luxury real-estate sales, interior decorating, event planning and 'client liaison' at [upscale auction houses].

"A not-so-incidental benefit of these glamour jobs is that they put women in the right circles to meet the next multimillionaire husband, if that's what they have in mind." Some of the women, the article went on to say, didn't date their clients until the job was finished, or the deal was closed.

Try the Internet. Surfing the Internet has become a bonanza for anyone who wants to find a partner.

For years, the women I know have complained that there are no men. On the Internet, you will find that that's not so. In fact, there are zillions of men! Zillions of them, sitting at their computers and looking for a relationship. You no longer have to go to a social situation and hope that the right person will find you in the room. Thanks to the Internet, you can access the world. You can meet people from anywhere around the globe or you can limit your search to people who are only blocks away. You can find people of every description, age, and interests. You're worried about meeting "strangers"? Meeting via the Internet isn't any different from meeting in a bar. Everyone is a stranger at first. Obviously, you take the usual precautions. You meet in a neutral place and size the person up; you go slowly in the first stages of the relationship until you get some sense of who and how legitimate the person is. But certainly you get your share of jerks and rats in conventional dating. And this is a lot better than sitting in your friend's house eating peanuts and complaining about the lack of guys. If you don't like "California Don" (they use nicknames), then you might like "Montana Matt," and if neither suits you, no problem, there are more. At the very least, you'll feel wonderful just discovering that life is full of possibilities, and there's a future for you. When I discovered the Internet, at first I felt like, "Men are falling from the sky! It's raining dates!"

—Pat, 42, makeup artist

I logged on to search for people in my area. I came upon a profile that looked interesting, and we wrote back and forth. Later in the day, I was going to meet my friends for a drink in a place that turned out to be convenient to both our homes. I e-mailed him to join us—it was safe, because my friends were coming and it was a place where people knew me—and we got acquainted. We continued our relationship via e-mail. Then I invited him to dinner when my children and some friends would also be there and asked him to install my scanner. He did, and we got to know each other. We married 19 months later.

—Dana, 50, artist

After thirteen years alone, I finally found him—my true soul mate. We are very much alike in our humor, thinking, life philosophy, even our looks. We were in love with each other before we even laid eyes on each other. We met via Digital City personal ads on AOL. I responded to his ad, he responded back. For the next four days we spoke on the phone every night for two to three hours. On the sixth day we met for lunch, and the rest is history. We both knew instantly that this was the person we'd been looking for all those years.

—Angela, 33, customer service representative

For those who think you only meet certain types of men over the Internet, let me tell you my experience. I met a plastic surgeon from an Ivy League school. He took my kids on a ski trip to Colorado and treated them to outfits and ski school. And for Valentine's Day, he took away some of my wrinkles and made my lips a little fuller. (My idea, not his; he said that he considered me perfect just as I was.)

—Lisa, 41, real estate broker

We typed to one another for a year and a half. Then he moved from the east coast to the west coast to have the love we had both had been searching for. (sigh)

—Wanda, 42, business owner

Become a volunteer. Some large cities have volunteer organizations specifically for singles. If they don't have one in your city, why not organize one yourself? It's a good excuse to call people, to get out in public, and to do something that is productive; and the chances of meeting interesting people are probably greater than in a bar.

Look all around you.

I met women at work, in bars, in the elevator. I'd constantly question the doorman of the building where I live: Who was that? Is she married? Is she seeing anyone?

—Bill, 47, foreign trader

You may only be attracted to one person out of twenty-five, or fifty, or one hundred, so you had better make it your business to meet as many people as possible. So you shouldn't rule out bars or dances. They're good meeting places. To make such outings comfortable, go with friends—and ask those friends to bring their friends. If you're concentrating on enjoying the company of your own group, you'll be more relaxed and approachable. Going as a couple—that is, with a friend of the opposite sex—can also be helpful.

Private parties are less of a hit-or-miss way of meeting people. Get together with friends, chip in to cover costs, and throw some parties yourself. Extending an invitation to a party is a great way to approach someone in whom you're interested, and being one of the hosts or hostesses gives you a good excuse to say hello to people you don't already know.

Sexuality and dating

Q: *What did you do wrong in looking for a husband?*
A: *I put out.*
Q: *What did you do right in looking for a husband?*
A: *I put out.*

—Haley, 54, headhunter

At what point do you begin a sexual relationship? People move more cautiously today than they did formerly, due to concerns about AIDS and other sexually transmitted diseases. Relationship advisor Sandra Harmon advises "No sex without commitment," and that may be the way to go.

I married my present wife because she was the only woman I ever met who didn't hop into bed with me. She said, "You want this, come get it at the altar." I think every guy wants to marry a virgin and most of us don't. We spend most of our lives trying to make sure the other guy doesn't get one either.

—Bob, 61, investor

Sex and the single parent

Dating presents a certain amount of difficulty for a single parent. Children continue to have the fantasy that their parents will get back together, which the "date" threatens. What's more, children have a great deal of trouble accepting their parents' sexuality. How they respond to new relationships depends on how old they are.

Younger children may not comprehend exactly what is going on, but they most likely still feel very connected to the biological parent who is not present (the ex) while they also feel proprietary about the custodial parent—two major strikes against the date. They may find it difficult, or even disgusting, to see a "stranger" behaving affectionately toward Mom or Dad. Adolescents, in the midst of defining their own sexuality, may be particularly uncomfortable, even appalled, to witness behavior that seems even remotely intimate.

"Wise parents behave discreetly. They don't have people they're dating stay in their home. They don't flaunt their relationship. They find ways to be together that are more private so they can set examples for their children," says Roxanne Permesly.

Know when to move on

The biggest mistake we make in dating is holding on too long. If it doesn't feel right, let go. If you're working too hard at a relationship, get out of it.

—Lee, 56, housewife

As women grow older, they may come to feel more insecure about their prospects for remarriage; often, they worry about losing their looks and know that, statistically, there are fewer men available to them. Having learned from their mistakes, they may be less likely to stay in a relationship that's wrong for them. But they may be tempted to stay too long in a relationship that's comfortable but stagnant.

Men may be less motivated than women to remarry: If they already have children, and particularly if they're the sole or primary breadwinner, a remarriage may mean additional burdens of responsibility they don't want. So, to protect herself, a woman should find out what her prospects are—because the deeper you get into the quicksand of an affair, the harder it is to pull out. If this were a job, after all, you wouldn't stay in a limbo of uncertainty forever—you'd ask for a raise or a promotion. So why would you waste years of your life in a dead-end romance?

But you can't ask about the future until you're sure that you're in a committed relationship—that is, you have become an integral part of one another's life; the people around you consider you a couple; you count on one another for affection and support; and you're comfortable revealing your feelings to one another. If you're at that point and your goal is remarriage, it's perfectly valid to ask, "Where do you think we're headed with this relationship?" or to state outright, "If a long-term relationship isn't something you're interested in, I don't want to go on." Once the words are uttered, stop talking and wait to hear the response. Do not make excuses and apologies for having brought up the issue, and resist the urge to say what you think he's feeling. Let your partner speak, if you want to learn how things really stand.

If your partner turns you down, is it irrevocable? Is he or she saying, "Let's wait a while," or making it clear that this relationship is not going to end in marriage? In the latter case, you may be crushed, but you shouldn't be angry. You should be glad that you had the courage to ask, and glad that your partner isn't simply stringing you along.

Because if you know this isn't the man or woman you'll be spending the rest of your life with, you can start looking for that person.

Keep your hopes up

"At Park Avenue tea parties, the popular theory is that a divorced woman has five years from the time her settlement comes through to meet the next husband. The deadline reflects the reality of modern divorce, which rarely grants a woman long-term alimony," reported *The New York Times* on June 27, 1999.

People who would like to remarry can be optimistic about their chances. Our survey confirms that most people find new spouses in less than five years: 14.9 percent of women and 19.2 percent of men paired up within a year; 27.5 percent and 28.6 percent, respectively, within two years, and 31.4 percent and 35.7 percent within three to five years. But 18.7 percent of women and 15.3 percent of men spent six to ten years being single, and 7.5 percent of women and 1.1 percent of men waited more than ten years to find the right person to remarry.

My first marriage lasted twenty years, and then I was single for nineteen years. Ironically, I had started a club in my city to introduce single people at dinner parties at fine restaurants. I hated the bar scene and thought it was degrading. I thought my club was a wonderful way to meet every single man in town in a civilized fashion. As a result, I met new men every day. Eighty people married as a result of my efforts, but I did not meet my own Prince Charming. I was the person pressing her nose against a window. But I knew in my heart I would meet the perfect man. I was never in love with anyone, and I wasn't looking for a particular type. It took me all nineteen years, and at last I found him. I am in love for the first time in my life and I am 63 years old. This man was worth waiting sixty years for.

—Anne, 63, real estate broker

3

HAVING SECOND
THOUGHTS

Q: What are you looking for in a partner?
A: Someone who won't divorce me.

—Florida man, 56, married three times

Suppose it's happened. The ink on your divorce papers has long since dried, you've found the right therapist, and you've put closure on the first marriage. You've been putting yourself back together: You're in great shape from working out at the gym, you've got a job that means something to you, you're juggling your social life and dealing with the kids, and you've even found a romance. And now—to your great astonishment—you're even thinking about remarriage.

Despite your happiness, you may have a lot of reservations. Are you ready to give up your new life and independence to move back into the confines of a marriage? Being unmarried, after all, is an option. And living as a single person really does mean never having to say you're sorry. As a single person, you rarely have to compromise about anything that's important to you, from the hours you keep to the way you run your house and discipline your children. A trait that may distinguish married people from unmarried people is their capacity to compromise. You may be unwilling to make all the compromises that are necessary.

Years ago, men and women who remained single were objects of gossip or pity, stereotyped as "confirmed bachelors" or "old maids," their sexuality a subject of speculation. Today, it's acceptable to find happiness solely in the company of your friends, your children (if you have any), and yourself. Millions of people do. Or, you may have a companion.

Going though life without an official partner may sometimes be lonely. But you have probably learned that, even when you are married, you may feel alone, and being half a couple doesn't make your life any less difficult.

I wish I had spent more time growing and figuring out what I really wanted before I decided to marry my current husband. I'm not saying that I wouldn't have chosen him if I had it to do all over again, I'm just saying that I've changed so much and have come so much into my own, I've realized that I didn't need to get married to find something to do with my life.

—Vicki, 40, music teacher

But even if you decide that remarriage is what you want, are you certain that this is the right person and the right relationship for the person you are now? Will love be lovelier the second time around? "In the first marriage," says therapist Roxanne Permesly, "people spend most of their time planning the wedding and the china patterns. For a second marriage, you should spend your time figuring out how to make the marriage work."

Is this the right person?

You come to your marriage with expectations based on your personal experience. Coming to a first marriage, your impressions are all secondhand—the sum total of what you observed as a witness to the marriage of your parents and other acquaintances and what you saw portrayed on television and in the movies. When you say "I do" a second or subsequent time, however, you carry along expectations which you acquired in the course of the marriage (or marriages) that you left behind.

Still, no marriage you have witnessed, nor any you have been part of, will provide an exact template for your next one. Chances are your new marriage will be better than the one that preceded it. Certainly it will be different in some ways.

One big difference between a first marriage and a remarriage is that people may not play traditional roles the second time around. This may take some adjustment. If you are a man who did all the financial planning in your previous marriage, you may have complained about having to take on so much responsibility. Yet, if you become involved with a woman who is used to managing her own affairs, you may find you have mixed feelings when she makes business decisions without consulting you. If you are a woman who has grown up with certain expectations about the role males should play, you may be accustomed to the man in your life taking on certain household chores. If your present partner cannot or will not do this, you may be disappointed and perhaps even annoyed.

The characteristics of remarriages vary wildly. Not only will your remarriage be different from your first one, it will be different from every other. Some remarriages come with surly teenagers, aging parents, and lots of dental bills. Others involve no children and include a hundred feet of oceanfront property and a well-funded retirement plan. However daunting or attractive these accompaniments are, they are not what determines how the marriage will go. While the absence or presence of stepchildren and/or financial security are important, the real key to a successful remarriage is how well the partners are suited to one another.

The only way to judge all the pluses and minuses that a new partner brings to a relationship, or whether the relationship itself will work out, is via the test of time. But there are many clues which can give you some indication of where you're headed. Whether or not you choose to take notice of them is another issue.

If you're happy with yourself and your life, you will meet another happy person and be in love. The really happy ones spot the unhappy ones and, no matter how strong the attraction, the red flags go up. They keep away because they know, "This one will be a problem."

—Louis, 46, small business owner

If only that were always so. But therapist Jill Muir Sukenick likes to quote the poet Edna St. Vincent Millay:

> . . . The heart is slow to learn
> What the swift mind beholds at every turn.

Typical reasons that people make bad partnership choices are that they focus more on getting married than on making sure they are marrying the right person; they have an unrealistic view of their relationship; they are repeating unhealthy patterns from the past; or they are marrying someone who is unsuitable in the hope that he or she will change.

Falling in love with marriage

I got engaged to my second husband while I was still married to my first. I didn't love him. I just loved being married. I just couldn't bear the idea of being single. After I got divorced, my friends told me that they nicknamed my second husband "Helen's purse." That's because he was about as noticeable as a purse tossed on a couch at a party. Someone would say, "Whose purse is that?" And someone else would say, "Helen's." Then, at the end of the party, I'd put "the purse" on my shoulder and take it home. Looking back on the marriage, I realize that was a pretty accurate description of what was going on. Of course, it took me a lot of therapy to recognize this.

—Helen, 58, writer

An obsession with the institution of marriage indicates that a person either feels incomplete or wants to prove to the world that someone finds her (or him) lovable because she/he fears that she/he is not. The sad result may be a marriage to someone who is not a true match in any way.

The one thing worse than not having someone in an essential job is having the wrong person in an essential job. That's kind of like marriage. It's bad to be lonely, but it's worse to be the companion of the wrong person.

—Jack, 65, lawyer

Some divorced men and women want the path of their married lives to continue, but with a different person as the copilot. Rather than act out of a real desire to be in an intimate relationship, they make a narcissistic choice: they find a person who is a mirror image of themselves or choose an idealized figure. Ultimately, someone following this pattern is unlikely to make a second, satisfying marriage and may go on to make multiple unsuccessful marriages.

Women who make multiple marriages may also be desperately looking for financial security.

When I married my second husband, I was trying to figure out where I was going to get my next meal. I found out the hard way: There's no money worth putting up with for that kind of marriage. But by the time

I met my third, I had a career, a house, a housemate to share expenses with. I didn't really need a husband. I'm sure that's why this one is working.

—Eleanor, 51, columnist

If they don't become independent, many women jump into—or remain in—any marriage, because they are terrified of having to depend on themselves for money.

My husband is wealthy but abusive. I've left him a couple of times, only to go back. I gave up my career and put my money into the marriage, so I felt strapped. Often I wish there weren't dollars and cents involved.

—Bev, 61, nurse

Most of the women who feel this way came of age prior to the 1970s and might not have had any preparation for a career or any lifetime goal other than marriage. And even in cases where a woman is capable of being economically self-sufficient—like the holder of "the purse," who earns well over $200,000 a year—if she was raised in a traditional family structure in which the father bore all the financial responsibilities, she may feel paralyzed by the prospect of managing without a husband.

Single men generally have an easier time socially and financially than single women, but there are other issues driving them to take on a spouse. They may want someone to take care of them and their children. Or, because men in general have more difficulty being intimate with others than women do, they often remarry to be sure they will have an attachment to someone. The specific woman is almost beside the point; what's important is that she exists to serve as a sounding board and loyal supporter. This is not a true relationship, because the husband in such a relationship talks *at* his spouse rather than with her. If he tires of her for whatever reason, he'll just replace her with a slightly different, equally receptive model.

Hanging on to the fantasy

Again, almost every person we talked to cautioned against rushing into a second marriage. You need time to meet and get to know everyone who is important in the life of your future spouse: the friends, the kids, the parents. More important, it takes time for you and your partner to know each other well.

In this marriage, I took time to discover what I was feeling each step of the way. I had a more mature outlook and more patience.

—Rebecca, 36, sales

When I remarried the second time, I forced myself to take it easy, be independent, and not be so anxious to include someone in my life so fast.

—Gwen, 48, school administrator

"Time in the literal sense is not the issue," says Sukenick. "What matters is whether you've had the opportunity in this relationship to move out of fantasy into reality. How clearly are you seeing your potential spouse? How does what's going on in this relationship compare to your relationships of the past? Did past relationships fail because you couldn't let go of a fantasy, and are you doing it again?"

We put on the Polo cologne or the designer shirt, and the woman puts on the makeup and lipstick and earrings and has her hair right, and that's who you see. It's a tribal dance. But once the dance is over, you have to paint the kitchen or get up in the morning, and you might not feel like putting on the tribal makeup. If you base a relationship on appearance only, it won't work. I've learned that marriage has to be unconditional. When you accept the other person for who he is and yourself for who you are, life will be easier. There won't be any tricks.

—Burt, 46, engineer

To love someone is to acknowledge and accept that person, warts and all. To truly know someone, you need to share experiences. Accumulating a large number of them will allow you to develop a bank of positive impressions and loving feelings that will sustain your relationship through difficult moments.

I spent a lot of time with my second husband over an eighteen-month period. My first husband and I married after knowing each other only six months, and I didn't see all of who he was. Abusive people are always super nice in the beginning.

—Dana, 50, artist

Rushing into marriage almost always results in disaster.

The first time, I had a six-week courtship and the marriage lasted ten miserable years. For my second, we waited a very long time. We've been together twenty years now.

—Faye, 45, songwriter

We dated a few years before we married. We had both been burned and didn't want to make the same mistakes again.

—Roberta, 53, government secretary

"What I'm finding," says family therapist Audrey Wentworth, "is that many people who remarry are already living together, sometimes as long as three to five years. From living together they were quite sure that who they were matched each other's expectations and that they could deal with the relationship. They didn't just discuss the issues, they lived them. Though where there are children involved, this isn't always possible."

Life is easy when things are going great, but you don't know if you're with the right person until issues start to come up. Anyone can put on a show for six months or even two years. If I could give any advice, it would be, "Take your time, don't rush to get married." When the hard times come, you'll see how someone handles pressure and how he behaves under the worst of circumstances. That's when you can really judge that person.

—Marcy, 37, designer

I think it's useful to live together first for a long, long time, and not rush to marry. You have to work a lot out when you get divorced, to learn a lot about yourself, to experience all the things you wanted to do and couldn't. I needed to have my independence while having a relationship. I think if I had remarried immediately I would have been back into the husband-taking-care-of-wife thing. I needed to have a feeling I was taking care of myself even though I was having companionship.

—Debbie, 58, social worker

Sometimes people who chose the wrong spouse the first time around have the fantasy that if they choose someone as unlike that first spouse as possible, the remarriage will be better. But it's immature to think you can base a relationship on the absence—or presence—of a single quality.

One of the reasons our marriage broke up was that she was very dour and repressed. She didn't enjoy sex. So when the marriage broke up, the one thing I wanted was a woman who loved sex. I found it, all right, but what I learned was that that gets old real fast. She would brag about my prowess, but that felt like competition. You can't build a marriage around that.

—Wally, 58, architect

This "Farewell, Dr. Jekyll, I'm in love with Mr. Hyde" hang-up is a losing proposition. When you look for someone who is the absolute opposite of your spouse—sexy versus staid, spontaneous versus stuffy—you may wind up with someone who lacks some of your former spouse's virtues. ("Stuffy" people are more likely to have steady paychecks than "spontaneous" people.) Another possibility is that you have so little objectivity that you think you've found someone very different when, in fact, you're marrying the same person all over again.

Repeating past mistakes

"Think of a remarriage as a second business. If your first business went bankrupt, would you go into that very same business over again?" asks psychiatrist Scott Permesly. It may not be rational to repeat the pattern of a bad marriage, but counselors see this "repetition compulsion" all the time.

Long ago, Sigmund Freud pointed out that people tend to re-create past experiences. Counselors see it all the time. "I had been seeing a divorced man who reported that his relationship with his ex-wife had been extremely hostile, with a lot of fighting. During one battle, the situation escalated to the point where there was a physical altercation," recalls Sukenick, for instance. "He started seeing another woman and they began having similar problems. He was very oppositional, and he tried to antagonize her in the same way that he had antagonized his spouse. He was headed down the same road."

It takes two! Your previous partner may indeed have been the major cause of the problems in your relationship, but generally the negative energy in a relationship doesn't come from only one source. The failure of a marriage is usually due to significant problems on both sides. Marriages that are a first for one of the partners statistically have a better chance of succeeding than marriages that are the second for both. Chances are that at least one spouse will not have a history of a conflict that she or he cannot resolve.

You can't have a good remarriage without first having had a good divorce. You will know you have "passed the divorce course" when you have put the blame and anger behind you, acknowledged and learned from your mistakes, and made positive steps to correct them. If you don't learn from your mistakes, you'll repeat them.

When my first husband left me for his secretary, I was devastated. I had just started my career. I wasn't financially secure and I felt unsure of myself in every area. I met my second husband six months later, and made a commitment to him much too soon. He was an alcoholic. During the ten years we were married, we went to therapy together, and I went alone. I was the only one doing the work. When I got married the third time, I was more aware of what to look for. And I didn't jump in this time. I realized that once you've developed strong feelings for someone, it's hard to walk away, even if you realize there's a problem. I definitely should have done more work on myself after my first marriage. I know what I want and what I won't put up with now, but that's only through strengthening my character through meditation and therapy.

—Gwen, 48, school administrator

Playing the hero

If you're privately thinking, This person drinks too much but when we get married, I'm going to change him and he's going to stop drinking, you had better run as far as you can in the other direction. You're not going to change the other person. The other person will have to change himself, and he will have to want to change. You don't have the control. Recognize that, and don't marry the person. Otherwise, you will wind up in divorce court because you're going to get so angry and frustrated. You have to marry the person you want, not someone you hope to mold into that person.

—Burt, 46, engineer

This is a "rescue fantasy," and it can be a continuing characteristic of people who played a similar role in their families of origin—rescuing a parent with problems, for example. Some people are professional rescuers, and carry this tendency to and from work with them.

I knew he drank too much but I thought I could change him. He had a drinking problem, but I was sure that was because nobody loved him. I was going to fix it. That's the nurse in me. He is an abusive drunk, and it's devastating. I've left him a couple of times, only to go back.
—Bev, 61, nurse

Another possibility is that the rescuers themselves have a fantasy of being rescued, and act it out in this manner.

A remarriage to someone with a serious abuse problem—someone who abuses drugs or alcohol, who gambles compulsively, or is emotionally abusive—is a blueprint for disaster. As the sober one in the relationship, you have to be realistic about its long-term prospects. Neither anger, shaming, blaming, or pleading—nor any amount of kindness—will get the person you're dealing with to change. They themselves will have to supply the motivation.

If you are not sure how serious the problem is, get more information. If you have never had any experience with someone who is a gambler, an alcoholic, or a drug abuser, you probably have no idea how to assess the degree of the problem or how difficult it would be to cope with. One thing is certain, though. The problem will inevitably get worse, because all those diseases are progressive. You'll need help.

Contact the offices of Alcoholics Anonymous, Narcotics Anonymous, or Gamblers Anonymous for information. (If you can't find the latter two in your area, Alcoholics Anonymous may be able to give you a referral or assistance. All of these groups use the same Twelve-Step program.) These organizations will help you find meetings for people whose partners have abuse problems. It's not enough to go to one meeting: You should attend at least ten of them before you decide whether or not they are helping you.

Our survey results showed that when a remarriage was less happy than the preceding ones, it was usually due to the fact that one partner had problems with abuse. To the question, "What is the greatest source of stress in your remarriage?" one such wife answered:

Husband denies alcoholism in his side of the family. Husband denies verbally abusive behavior. Husband is dishonest and narcissistic. A successful marriage depends on one word: trust. I do not feel it anymore.
—Marianne, 56, realtor

Other bad choices

Certain remarriage scenarios are destined to fail.

I had been married and divorced very young. I was in my early twenties when I met my husband. We were going to start by just living together but my mother-in-law was from a very traditional Italian family and she said there's no way a son of mine is going to be living with someone. So before you knew it, we were planning an extravaganza of a wedding. The marriage didn't last a year.
—Leslie, 47, therapist

Sadly, the "Please-the-Parents Pairing" is only one of a myriad of types of remarriages which are doomed from the start. Other types follow.

So There! People whose egos were badly shattered by the breakup of a former marriage may marry for revenge or simply to prove (to themselves and everyone else) that they are desirable. Such a marriage is burdened by underlying neediness, hostility, and anger.

Two Wrongs Don't Make a Rite People whose affair broke up a marriage may marry one another even though their relationship doesn't have the glue to make it last.

The "Romantic Isle Illusion," also known as the "Club Med Misun-

derstanding" The couple meets in an atmosphere conducive to a torrid, romantic liaison, and they mistake their affair for a serious relationship.

The Spotted Leopard Syndrome This happens when you believe that someone who behaved badly with a former spouse is going to be much nicer to you. When you fall in love with someone who has had a failed marriage, it is tempting to become an ally and blame all his or her problems on the former mate. But pay attention to what you're hearing. You may get a preview of what's in store for you!

Phillip had been previously married to a woman who, at the time they got together, had six children—all under 8 years old! He subsequently adopted them all, and the family was intact for another ten years. Yet, by the time we were together, he had no relationship with any of them. It is easy to rationalize away the fact that a person has lost touch with a stepchild . . . or even two. But you do have to say to yourself—as I finally did—what kind of a person couldn't find one of six children to bond with? I did marry him, and when the marriage broke up after ten years, he abandoned my children, too.

—Helen, 58, writer

Have you learned from the past?

Having been married is like other major life experiences, such as having a baby or buying a house: Once you've done it, you're much smarter about anticipating problems and creative about finding solutions the next time. From then on, you will have a good sense of when a marriage may be going wrong and at least some sense of what is required to make it right.

Also, when contemplating a remarriage, you're older and wiser than you were before. You're less likely to be impetuous and, while you may feel lustful, you're less likely to be driven by lust. Most people we surveyed who entered into a remarriage told us that their decision to remarry, unlike the decision they made in a prior marriage, was made using both their head *and* their heart.

You should have learned, as well, that the relationship will not be without problems and issues and will not satisfy all your needs. It is very unlikely that you will find one person who can be all things to you.

I think people work harder at a remarriage because you realize how awful it is to go through a breakup and a divorce. You value marriage, and you realize it takes two people to make it work. Your expectations are not the same. You know it's not always perfect.

—Emily, 57, insurance adjuster

Togetherness and independence

A first marriage is likely to be a pairing of two underdeveloped personalities who have come together in order to complete one another's deficits. A remarriage is more likely to represent the coming together of two independent people who plan to entwine, rather than merge, their lives.

In marriages between mature people with a variety of interests there's likely to be less dependency on a spouse to meet all of each other's companionship needs—for going to the theater or golf course, shopping or fishing. Instead of being resentful or frustrated you'll find a way to meet those needs elsewhere. It's important to negotiate this before you marry.

We should have discussed [the fact that] I want more time by myself, and he wants more time with me. This is a big conflict.

—Maggie, 54, lawyer

A mature partner shouldn't consider your occasional need for other companionship, or for privacy and solitude, to be a threat or an insult. And vice versa.

I have my own business, and I work long hours. I was so scared that my new husband would feel that I should be there, at home with him, at the end of the day. Or that if he went off to the country for a weekend, I would have to go with him, no matter what. And I was so relieved that he didn't feel we had to be joined at the hip and that he didn't make the same demands on me that husband number one made.

—Roslyn, 55, book editor

In my first marriage, if my husband said he wanted to go off for some time alone, I was threatened. I would say, "Why do you want to go away from me?" I guess it was an abandonment issue. [In my second marriage,] because of my counseling, I know that the world isn't going to cave in if we aren't attached to each other's hip. We don't live out of each other's pockets. We know we have to have our own time alone and our own private space. I get a lot of pleasure out of knowing that we are independent and we are joined as well.

—Roberta, 53, government secretary

You learn that needing some space doesn't mean you don't love your partner—and that companionship may warrant some compromises.

After I divorced I felt I'd gained a measure of freedom, and now that I've married my second wife, I don't have it anymore—but the older you get, the more you feel as if it's not so good to be permanently alone. Sometimes I think if she doesn't get out of my space, I'm going to run away. But when she does go away, I can't stand to be without her.

—Jack, 65, lawyer

Great expectations

We discussed nothing ahead of time.
　　　　　　　　—Woman in an unhappy, abusive remarriage

Many of the people we talked to said they weren't matched well the first time around, but in their remarriage they had found a true companion.

It was fated for my second husband and me to be together. We are from different parts of the country but we have a great deal in common. The first time, I got married to a man with whom I was incompatible. It's as simple as that. Nothing I know now would have changed my first marriage [because it simply wasn't the right one for me].
　　　　　　　　—Rita, 45, college professor

All couples make a number of unspoken agreements before they marry, in every area that must be negotiated—from who does what chores, to who gets the main vote in financial decisions, to how often they have sex. Many first marriages break up because of major misunderstandings about where the partners stand on critical issues, either because these thoughts weren't expressed beforehand or because someone wasn't being honest.

I got married too young. I never sat with my first wife and talked about, What do you expect from me? What do you expect about children? What do you want our life together to be?
　　　　　　　　—Wally, 58, architect

When these expectations are actually put into words, the marriage may be more successful.

We literally sat down and made lists together of what we liked to do. We had a lot of common goals, even that we both wanted to marry outside our professions.

—Louis, 46, small business owner

While situations can change and opinions may be swayed, you and your partner probably stand a better change of success if you start your marriage sharing the same expectations about deeply important matters such as children, financial goals, career plans, life-styles, sexuality, and intimacy.

Children: to have or have not

The usual difference in age between a husband and wife in a first marriage is two years. But in a remarriage between a divorced man and a single woman, there is often a greater gap. So it's fairly common to have a situation in which a man has already had the experience of being a parent and is totally opposed to having more children for a variety of reasons: He may not have the financial means to support two families. He may be concerned about being too old to raise a young family. He may want a life-style unencumbered by parental obligations, particularly the overwhelming ones of raising infants and small children. He may feel guilty about the prospect of making the children of his former marriage feel displaced by a new family. Or he may have found that the responsibilities of parenthood outweighed its joys. A young wife, on the other hand, may seriously resent being denied the opportunity to be a mother.

A major component in the breakup of our marriage was my long-standing resentment over his lack of cooperation in having a child. I had trouble conceiving, and he agreed to see a fertility specialist only after I prodded him endlessly. Then, even though he was theoretically cooperating, he would sabotage the process. He would "make a collec-

tion," as he called it, on a day when I wasn't fertile, or he'd leave the test tube at the wrong temperature. Eventually he owned up to the truth: He was satisfied with the two sons he had from a previous marriage and didn't really want any more children. How could I forgive him?

—Cyndi, 55, publicist

Some men rule out having children in any marriage under any circumstance, because parenthood is incompatible with their life-style.

I divorced my ex-wife over the children issue. She's a lovely woman, but we just weren't headed to the same place. She wanted a very traditional life-style, and she wanted kids. I told her that was okay with me, but then she'd have to choose between the kids and a career, because I didn't want any children of mine to be raised by a nanny. Well, she agreed to that plan, and she geared up for that. She stayed home more, did the gourmet-cooking thing, acted like a housewife, and basically became—ironically, in an effort to please me—a person I had absolutely no interest in being married to. I didn't care about her hearthside skills, I didn't want to be a father. I wanted a partner who could be with me, out and about, someone to share my life-style. We parted amicably. My present wife is a career woman, eager to go all the places I want to go to, and exactly the kind of person I want to be with.

—Robert, 59, businessman

When a woman who is already a mother marries a man with no children, usually she is willing to have a child together if that is his wish. Since she has already made a commitment to motherhood and understands what it entails, whatever problems that might ensue tend not to be particular to a remarriage.

But there are some women who prefer to remain childless.

Before my first marriage, I had decided I didn't want a family. But I didn't want to admit this to my fiancé. He came from a large Italian family, had been raised in the Catholic faith, and dreamed of many children. I thought he would be so happy married to me that he would let go of the dream of having children. Instead, he was devastated and he accused me of tricking him. Because of his deep religious conviction, he really couldn't stay married to me. Eventually, he filed for an annulment. I'm still young enough to have kids, so it's certainly possible I could wind up dating another guy who wants to start a family. But I'll be more honest from the start. I won't be afraid to say what I want. If that's not what he wants, then I guess he's not the one for me.

—Alice, 36, massage therapist

If you have the courage to put your cards on the table, you may move the relationship forward—or you may end it. But at least you're making your goal clear and avoiding major crises later on.

I decided to get married again because on our second or third date she said to me, "I want to have a baby, and if that's not where you're headed, let's not go out anymore, so I can get on with my life and try to meet a man who wants what I want." I thought about it, and I realized that she was the one. I said okay.

—Louis, 46, small business owner

The lesson from all these cases is to be candid about your real expectations and ask your partner to do the same. You may be afraid that hearing the truth will ruin the relationship, but if you aren't honest, it's unlikely to last anyway. Dealing with children that either of you may already have is a complex issue. See Chapters 4 and 7.

Money: what's your bottom line?

"You can be as romantic as you please about love . . . but you mustn't be romantic about money," wrote George Bernard Shaw. Though people may be eye-poppingly candid about volunteering the most intimate details of their sex lives, if the conversation turns to money it's quite a different matter. We are culturally conditioned to be secretive about our money and if we feel we're expected to disclose how much we earn or how we spend it we tend to clam up. Asking about it directly seems terribly rude or pushy, and it's not always possible to gauge people's financial situation by the size of their home or the make of their cars. But it's an issue you must explore if the person in question is a prospective mate.

Chapter 5 describes the detailed financial planning that ought to take place once you have decided to get married. Before that, while you are still assessing a relationship's prospects, you should explore your general attitudes about money and the feelings about money instilled in you by your families. Do you come from a family of spenders or savers? Did you have to work to earn your allowance or pay your way through college? How much credit card debt can you tolerate? Are you and your prospective partner in basic agreement about the life-style to which you aspire? *The New York Times* quoted a young woman who had a good sense of how to coax out this information: "My expectations about what I want out of life are high. And before I became really involved with someone I wanted to know if we were thinking the same way. I just had no interest in being with someone who isn't driven. He didn't have to be Donald Trump, but I wanted to be with someone who can hold his own and also has similar values. Of course you have to dance around a little to fish out the information. I hint. [I'd say what I'd like to do if I won the lottery, or I'd say that my goal is to make enough to put in the bank and retire with $50,000 income a year. I'd ask what his dreams were.]"

Having a similar goal about the kind of life-style you want or the size of the nest egg you're aspiring to is only half the issue. You need to know what you're willing to do to get there. Some people are willing to live on a tight budget until they have accumulated a large nest egg. Others prepare for the future by making high-risk investments.

People typically polarize around the subject of money, falling at either one extreme or the other: fearful or fearless; hoarder or spender; pragmatist ("Show me the money") or romantic ("Tell me your dream").

I was stunned to discover that we had completely different agendas. She wanted to use both our incomes to buy a fancy house, but my plan was to spend one income only and put the other aside, just in case either of us ever wanted to leave work.

—Norman, 53, manufacturer

Hoarders do well together, but a pair of spenders is a recipe for disaster. The saver/spender combination is most typical and, unless the extremes are too great, it can work. If the saver and the spender are miles apart, they may exacerbate each other's bad habits. The more careless a spender becomes, the tighter a hoarder draws the purse strings. And if the hoarder becomes increasingly penny-pinching, the spender throws money around more freely.

Having incongruent attitudes will affect many areas of your relationship. If your partner classifies some of the things that are important to you as frivolous or unnecessary expenses, or if you feel shamed and guilty even about spending money that is yours, arguments and resentments will result.

Being in a nontraditional relationship in which the woman is the primary wage earner or has the lion's share of holdings can also create problems in a remarriage if the partners aren't comfortable in those roles. The traditional pattern for marriage has been that the man brought the money to the relationship and the woman brought the nurturing and sexuality. That was a convenient exchange because until recently women couldn't get power except through men, and before the sexual revolution men couldn't get sex without marriage. Not so long ago the few examples of role reversal were usually unhappy alliances, such as when heiress Doris Duke was taken advantage of by playboy Porfirio Rubirosa. But today many women are in a position of power and can bring status and money to a relationship with a man who has chosen a different type of life-style. Such a relationship can work out so long as each partner completely understands his or her role and does not expect things to change—that is, the woman does not harbor a notion that the man will become her financial caretaker, and he has no ego problems and continues in his role of being loving and supportive.

We haven't [had] a lot of problems on the economic side because I'm financially independent. I can afford to support my kids and I have done so for years because their father is an alcoholic and irresponsible. I was used to standing alone, and I didn't look to my second husband as a provider. He earns a modest living, and his company health insurance covers us. He also contributes something toward the maintenance of the house, and throws extra into the pot when his kids come to stay. I made a conscious decision that I wanted emotional support in this marriage and the financial support was not important.

—Donna, 40, textile designer

Anyone who claims that he or she can "rise above" all the financial issues in remarriage is not being 100 percent truthful. This kind of statement usually comes from the one who is perceived to have the money in the relationship. He or she is either keeping the true amount of his or her money secret in order to protect it from the other person, or he or she is doing so out of fear that the partner-to-be will find out there is less money than rumored. Either way, the attitude signals that the relationship is not truly intimate.

Career: who works and until when

A husband and wife may have different expectations about her career. She may want to take time off to raise a family while he, on the other

When you're The Odd Couple

For me, the hardest thing about my second marriage was sharing a bathroom. Growing up, my brother and I had separate bathrooms. When I was married the first time, we had our own bathrooms. For fifteen years, I was single, with my own bathroom. Then, all of a sudden, I was sharing a bathroom. The steam drove me crazy.

—Roslyn, 55, book editor

Do you roll up the toothpaste tube or do you squeeze at random? How orderly are you? How do you intend to split the chores? Remarried spouses are older and more likely, therefore, to be creatures of habit. Can you foresee any adjustments that it would be hard for you to make? Having lived in a marriage before, you should know how to prioritize what's important, and what can simply be put aside.

I learned a lot of things in the course of my first marriage. A lot of the little things that annoyed me I thought were things [only] my wife did. I used to think she was just picky. And then I learned, in this second marriage, that some of that stuff was just the kind of things women do—little things, like paying attention to how you dressed, what you were wearing and when. Both my wives wanted to pack for me. I used to think it was strange, then I got used to it. But it's not a guy thing, that's for sure. The last thing a man would say is, "Darling, can I pack for you?"

—Karl, 58, inventor

Arguing over trivia is frustrating and embarrassing. You feel silly, because these disagreements seem so contrary to the idea of romantic love. But there are reasons for them. The particular incident or behavior that bothers you—the hair in the sink, the steam on the mirror—is probably a trigger for other issues. When you stumble over underwear draped all over the floor or discover that the last of the toilet tissue has been used up and the roll hasn't been replaced, you're not just annoyed at the lack of order—you're annoyed because you see the incident as a sign that your needs aren't respected and therefore that you aren't valued.

Instead of dismissing or suppressing your feelings, have a discussion about what you need and want. If it's clear that you're struggling over issues that indicate deeper problems, you may need a counselor to sort them out. And if the issues reveal very different value systems, maybe that's something to consider when deciding whether or not you really want this marriage.

Intimacy, fidelity, and sexuality

After gathering experience in a first marriage, a person usually has a better idea of the importance of sexuality and of his or her needs.

For my second husband, I picked someone who I thought would be loyal and with whom I felt secure. But most important, I felt a strong passion for him, too. With my first husband, I didn't feel that, and I was always beating myself up for wanting that passion and feeling guilty, feeling that maybe I was too demanding.

—Tara, 36, housewife

I married at the age of 21 in an era when most women married the first man they had sex with. I was no exception. With no basis of comparison, I attempted to find sexual fulfillment. I couldn't have orgasms right away, and my husband was not supportive. He wasn't very interested in sex at all. We had sex maybe twice at month, usually at my initiation, and naturally I assumed he was not attracted to me. When I divorced at 27, I was insecure and unsure of myself sexually. However, when I did become involved in a relationship, it became apparent that my ex-

husband was the one with the problem. Most of the men I dated were interested in sex, and I had a three-year relationship with a man who had a voracious sexual appetite. That was what I needed, and it helped heal the pain of my divorce and put things in the proper perspective. I could then go forward and, with my repaired self-esteem, find what was good for my needs. After ten years of being single, I remarried. I had experience and maturity and knew what I wanted in a partner sexually. It was important for me to find a man with whom I had great sex and who enjoyed it as much as I did. That was my personal need and desire, and I refused to settle for less.

—Tanya, 52, interior decorator

Whether you did or did not have experience with an adulterous partner in your past marriage—but especially if you did—you should discuss your expectations about fidelity. If a monogamous relationship is important to you but not what your partner has in mind, better to find out sooner rather than later. Determine whether your partner will say, "I won't," before you say, "I do."

Resolving disagreements

How will you deal with conflicts? "Often you may repeat the style you observed from your parents," says psychologist Holli Bodner. Both protracted, stony silence and frequent emotional outbursts are difficult to endure and don't move you toward resolution. A partner who is committed to your relationship should agree to get help for the problems which you yourselves cannot work out before and in the course of your remarriage.

I went to therapy alone, and then my husband-to-be and I went to therapy together, but I felt for sure we wouldn't get out of it together. I thought the relationship wouldn't last, that he would say, "This woman is so screwed up that I want nothing to do with her." But my desire to change my life was so important to me. I didn't want to make a mistake. I needed to know that if it wasn't going to be right, I should find out before I committed to it. I'd rather go to therapy and decide that we shouldn't be together than go through another divorce. I'd rather be alone than make a mistake.

—Marcy, 37, designer

4

IT'S A PACKAGE DEAL

My husband came into our marriage with so much baggage that he needed a porter.

—New York woman, 52, married once

Why remarriages fail

Many remarriages don't work out because the couple is fundamentally incompatible. They may have insurmountable personality conflicts or unrealistic expectations about the marriage. Or they may have just married the wrong person for the wrong reasons at the wrong time.

Or the couple cannot free themselves of the grief and loss associated with past relationships and so are unavailable for a new one. If you have not brought closure to a past relationship, any new relationship will remind you of your previous feelings of loss, pain, and failure. You may not even be conscious of these feelings, and/or you may not have the skills, or seek the professional help, that can help you to deal with these feelings. But if the issues from a previous marriage are not completely resolved, it will be difficult to solve current conflicts.

I am married to a widower and I have not been able to overcome the insecurities and uncertainties in this relationship. I think it is much more difficult than being married to a divorced man.

—Lois, 43, literary agent

I had never been married, and at 39 I was thrilled to fall in love with a man whose previous wife had died. We got along beautifully, but right after we married and for no apparent reason, he began to pull back. He was less affectionate. He held back with his emotions and his thoughts. He didn't even want to share experiences anymore. He became sedentary and only wanted to stay at home. I was obsessed with the thought that I wasn't good enough for him. Fortunately, we both went into therapy and discovered that he hadn't mourned the loss of his wife enough. He couldn't forgive himself for replacing her, and he took out that anger on me, but his rage had nothing whatsoever to do with who I was.

—Rhonda, 47, 911 operator

Before taking on the additional issues in the remarriage "package," a couple should address potential hazards in their own relationship.

The ghosts of marriages past

"Some people say that to see how a man will treat you in a marriage, look at how he treats his mother. In a second marriage, perhaps you should look at how he treats his ex-wife," says psychotherapist Jill Muir Sukenick.

Shortly after I met my husband, he introduced me to his former wife, with whom he has a cordial relationship. In fact, he is the one who introduced her to her present husband. My opinion of him went up a few notches when I saw how civilized he was with his ex. I know very well that you can't always get along with a former spouse—I've personally burned the bridges to my past husbands—but when someone does [continue to be cordial to his former spouse], I always think it's a mark in his favor. I felt he was a person of consistency and good judgment. While he and the ex might not have been good as husband and wife, clearly he never did anything so terrible that she never wanted to see him again, and I saw that he chose a person whom he continues to respect.

—Harriet, 53, freelance journalist

Unfortunately, there are relatively few such pleasant stories. "You have to be a very robust type of person to take on a man with children and a hostile ex-wife," says psychologist Holli Bodner. But when you get involved with a formerly married man, a hostile woman may well come with the package. For some of the people we surveyed, that would be cause to back off.

I would only remarry someone who has never been married before. It has been a wake-up call, dealing with this problem, and I would not want to do it again.

—Yvonne, 34, medical technician

The issues of damaged self-esteem that people bring from a broken marriage may have an even more profound impact on a potential relationship. If you or your spouse had a history of disappointments in a prior marriage—which is very likely the case, or the marriage would be intact—that unfinished business will carry forward. Though the problems it creates may not be evident in the early stages of your new relationship, they will arise sooner or later.

Open up. You and your partner have a better chance of making a healthy remarriage if you can talk freely to one another about your past marital history.

One of the few people we heard from in an unhappy remarriage said that the central issue she faced was her partner's unresponsiveness.

The biggest stress is his lack of compassion and understanding for my fears and concerns from my first marriage.

—Sarah, 37, consultant

You may feel slighted and alone as a result of being "frozen out" like this, and a failure to communicate about significant issues poses the larger danger that you will project your own meanings onto each other's behavior. You may presume that you know what your partner is thinking, based on what you yourself are thinking, and then, when you react according to the scenario that you have created, in effect, your partner—and his or her thoughts—no longer exists. Only your idea of that person exists, which leads to distortion and conflict.

I was in an elevator that stalled briefly. A stranger walked in just before the doors closed and said, jokingly, "Were you holding it for me?" Also joking, I said, "Yes; I was hoping you'd show up." He said, "You'd settle for anyone, huh?" I immediately felt defensive: I wondered if I seemed unattractive or desperate for a man. Then I realized he was being defensive also, surprised that I would "settle" for him. I realized how that same kind of misunderstanding can play out in our family situations.

—Elisa, 42, publicist

"If your partner is still harboring extreme anger toward the ex, consider that a red flag of warning for your own relationship," says psychiatrist Scott Permesly. In most cases, someone who had particular problems in a prior relationship—for example, if the ex-spouse mishandled money and debt, couldn't hold onto a job, had extramarital flings, or was an alcoholic—is very likely unconsciously to make a new partner into the old spouse and react to, or try to change, any behavior that they see as part of a pattern, based on their past experience.

An impulsive purchase by the current spouse may trigger a host of critical comments or accusations of being careless about money from the partner who was once married to a spendthrift. If your partner had been married to someone with a bad employment history and heard you criticize your boss or your job, he or she might challenge the validity of the complaint or warn you about job security. Your unexpected lateness or an unexplained phone call may trigger stony silence or angry confrontation from someone whose ex engaged in extramarital affairs.

Being subjected to too much criticism and irony by a previous partner will make some people hypersensitive. An offhand or amusing comment from you may appear to them to be a veiled insult. If his or her former spouse controlled the family with bouts of explosive anger, the person you're involved with may be excessively defensive. A person whose partner died may be excessively fearful of another loss and become overanxious concerning a new partner's health habits.

It is not unusual to have certain insecurities about being as attractive, talented, or successful as a prior spouse or to worry about your partner's lingering romantic or sexual feelings toward the ex. And sometimes, rather than live down the legacy of a previous partner, you have to live up to it. A widow or widower may attribute extraordinary virtues to a former spouse. Whether such qualities truly existed doesn't really matter, but they may seem difficult or impossible for a new spouse to measure up to.

Inge Morath, a professional photographer known for her evocative portraits, is also, as *The New York Times* put it, "famously married" to playwright Arthur Miller. Mr. Miller, of course, was himself once "famously married" to actress and renowned sex symbol Marilyn

Monroe. "Matrimonially speaking, wasn't Marilyn Monroe a hard act to follow?" a reporter asked.

"I knew about our feelings," said Ms. Morath, suggesting why it was not difficult for her to follow in Monroe's footsteps. "I never had this film star admiration. And you know, I had plenty of good boyfriends, too."

It takes a very secure person to surmount issues that linger from the past and threaten to intrude on the present relationship.

I was very scared about making a commitment for the second time. It was very hard for me to trust again because my first husband walked out on me.

—Emily, 57, insurance adjuster

We had a painful marriage and a painful divorce, so I was not a trusting person when I met my current husband. My ex could make $100,000 a year and spend $200,000. [Extravagant spending] was a hot button for me.

—Darcy, 43, housewife

My reservation in my current (third) marriage is that there could be another huge surprise. I have already been through enough. My second husband, who knew I had gone through my first husband's struggle with alcoholism, didn't tell me he was a recovering addict until after we were married.

—Gwen, 48, school administrator

My first marriage wasn't good and he never tried to please me. It took me a long time to get over the expectation that my second husband would inevitably react with anger the way my first husband did.

—Beth, 53, office manager

Communicating your concerns can help both of you to enlist one another's support so you can help each other put these issues to rest.

My ex-wife turned out to be a liar and a flake. She would take off sometimes, and just leave me a note. I put up with a lot because I didn't know how not to put up with it. When I dated my second wife, I explained to her my sensitivity to deception or any hint she was unreliable or unstable. I knew that I would overreact if she did things that reminded me of my first wife.

—Irv, 48, plastics manufacturer

I have to watch myself comparing my ex and this husband—both negatively and positively. My current husband sometimes looks at me and says, "What? Do you think I'm acting like him?" and I'll say, "I sort of was thinking that." You have to learn to start over and separate and not always be comparing.

—Karen, 51, writer

No relationship is static. During your courtship, and, if you remarry, during the marriage itself, both people must continually reassess themselves and one another so that the relationship can grow. As you become more and more intimate, you can become aware of one another's insecurities and fears and become a source of reassurance and comfort.

My husband had fallen in love with another woman, so we divorced. I remarried relatively soon afterward. I was still young and very pretty, and I'm sure to most people I seemed very secure. But one episode early in our relationship showed me how well my husband understood me and knew what I needed from him. We were at a party and he was talking to a woman friend of both of ours. I was in no way jealous of her—not consciously, anyway—but I kept drifting over to my husband, asking him to dance, even though he was clearly engrossed in conversation. The third time I interrupted him, he excused himself for a moment, turned away from the woman, and looked me full in the face. "It's okay, honey," he said. "I love you." He gave me a hug and then turned back to her. And really, he understood what I needed. I didn't need to dance: I just needed his reassurance and acknowledgment because I was feeling insecure.

—Ellen, 54, university professor

It's bigger than both of you

Still, no matter how perfectly you and your spouse-to-be are suited for one another, there are other factors to consider before you pledge your troth.

A first marriage is a merger of two people who bring together two sets of family experiences, traditions, and habits. In a second marriage, the number and complexity of these relationships may increase exponentially. The resulting "megafamily," as some sociologists term it, may include ex-partners of both spouses, children from past marriages, extra sets of grandparents, step-aunts and uncles, half-siblings, and others.

The more eager you are to remarry and start over again, and the more convinced you are that you are well suited to one another, the more optimistic and hopeful you probably are that whoever else is affected by your decision will go along with your plans and share your enthusiasm.

But the complicated, often conflicting needs of all these interrelated people are rarely, if ever, congruent with your fantasies and needs, or with those held by your partner or those you hold as a couple. Since you and your proposed spouse are happy to have found one another, you doubtlessly would prefer the people around you to feel as you do, that it's wonderful you'll be together. But some of them may still not have gotten past the turmoil of the divorce or death that ended the prior marriage. Among the emotions that they may experience are a sense of loss, anxiety about change, anger, frustration, hurt, and abandonment—all of which can cause regressive and troublesome behavior.

That's why it is not enough to consider only your compatibility with your partner when you assess the chances of success for a second marriage. Remember that your potential spouse comes as a package deal with other relationships, and the shadows of his or her past will be cast on your future. You cannot anticipate or solve all the issues that will come up once the marriage has taken place, but you can make yourself aware of them and anticipate how you will deal with them.

How children will affect your remarriage

In the case of former spouses, you're dealing with ghosts. But if children are part of a proposed remarriage, you'll be dealing with very substantial beings. Legacies of the past, they will become very much a part of your present and future.

In 1994, one expert estimated that 1300 new blended families were forming every day. According to the Stepfamily Foundation, the U.S. Census Bureau predicted that by the year 2000, more Americans would be living in stepfamilies than in traditional nuclear families.

Raising children puts a strain on every resource, from time, space, money, and patience to goodwill. No doubt this is why one source estimates that 60 percent of stepfamilies in the United States break apart within ten years of their founding. Reviewer Sue Gaisford, writing about Joanna Trollope's novel *Other People's Children* in *Harpers & Queen,* points out that, "You may rearrange and resettle them, but children do not readily relinquish or replace a parent, however unsatisfactory the original. Similarly a stepmother may well love her new husband more than she even likes his children. . . . The [book's] argument is that the success of a second marriage depends heavily on the sensitivity with which the children are handled."

Being alert to the underlying issues

Understanding the sources of potential problems will help you make whatever adjustments are necessary so that everyone can move past these obstacles. Not being prepared means one or both of you may stumble.

Suppose, for example, you're a woman whose future stepdaughter creates a scene at the dinner table and then storms out of the room. Her distress may be a reaction to the fact that someone else is sitting in her mother's customary place; but as a stepparent, you may take offense or feel hurt for reasons that relate to your own history. If your parents were a "closed corporation," you may have felt you were an intruder in their presence, so you don't feel entitled to a place in similar situations. People give their own meaning to experiences, creating distortions that create major or irreparable rifts. But if everyone attempts to understand the dynamics, they can talk about situations that arise and gain clarity about each other's perceptions. Rather than hitting a wall, you will have charted a pathway to communication.

Entering a remarriage is like walking onto a movie set long after the filming has begun. The other cast members have to adjust to a new presence *and* to the fact that the script may have to be rewritten. *You* have to find a way to fit yourself into a story line and mood that's already been established. These adjustments are difficult for everyone. As Freud has noted, people are resistant to change. Even when change is for the better, it is often associated with loss.

A therapist told my former husband and me that there are two ways to come into a remarriage where there are children. You can come in as a visiting professor of anthropology, get to know the people and appreciate how they run their lives. Or you can come in as a colonialist, ready to condescend, feeling that the people you're visiting are doing everything the wrong way and you can set it right.

—Darryl, 51, retailer

Questions to be addressed

There are many practical decisions to be made regarding the children as you contemplate remarriage.

If both children and stepchildren are involved, will it be possible to treat them equally? If there is a big disparity between the incomes of the father and the stepfather (or even between the biological parents and the step-grandparents), the children of one former marriage may be indulged with costly vacations and generous allowances while the children of the other will be expected to get jobs and student loans if they want a college degree. Tremendous rivalries and resentments may occur. These financial issues should be resolved before the remarriage (see Chapter 5). Treating the children equally in emotional terms will be an even greater problem.

He was fiercely loyal to his two children and he didn't have enough maturity or space in his heart for mine. He was trying to make sure his children were taken care of, to make up for their mother leaving them, and also to make up for the fact that he thought he'd neglected them while she was present. He was jealous of my attention to my kids.
                                                        —Lynda, 54, therapist

Do you agree about fundamental issues of discipline and indulgence? Would your prospective spouse deal with your children in an acceptable way? And how would you deal with his/her children?

How comfortable do your children seem to be with this person? A man who makes you feel wonderful about yourself may have the opposite effect on a child. A woman who is tender and caring may be awkward and distant in her role as stepmother. Naturally, there is a certain amount of awkwardness to be expected during the period of adjustment, but sometimes you can see underlying attitudes that may never be properly overcome. Either your marriage or your relationship with your children will suffer—or both.

My daughter, like me, tended to be plump. For my girlfriend, who is model-thin, weight is a big issue. When my daughter visited us for the weekend, my girlfriend watched everything she ate, and served her dinners she hated: fish and vegetables, no starch, no dessert. It was as if my daughter's weight would somehow reflect on her. I loved this woman but I couldn't see living in a situation where my kid was having her self-esteem constantly eroded.

—Noel, 53, sports manager

I married a woman with a couple of kids, and my own kids were living with their mother. There was friction between my children and her, and her position was, you married me, so I should come first. The marriage broke up and it was years before I repaired the damage with my children.

—Wally, 58, architect

Being alert to what's ahead

One remarried woman told us, "Spend at least one holiday season with your fiancée's children before making that final commitment. If you don't like them, you may want to bail out immediately. Things only get worse."

The daunting physical demands of raising young children may seem overwhelming. With older children, the difficulties are more likely to be psychological. Yet few people are deterred from a marriage by the prospect of difficulties with stepchildren, even when the specter of future troubles is staring them in the face.

I've never been married before, and I'm engaged to a woman who has a 13-year-old daughter. Not only do I not love this child, but most of the time, I don't even think I like her. Naturally, her mother is her constant defender. She says things like, "She's just a kid. She doesn't mean anything by her behavior." We almost broke up over these arguments, but instead we went to couples counseling. I'm still getting married, though I am very aware we have a problem. I'm hoping time will heal it.

—Sean, 39, retail sales

And some problems may not be foreseen—for example, the difficulty of being an intimate participant in the child's relationship with your spouse. As parent and child, they may have developed ways of interacting that you don't approve of or that make you uncomfortable—such as shouting matches or stormy outbursts. You may not be enthusiastic about witnessing their struggles.

I had a lot of concern about the fact that she still had a young daughter at home. We'd all be living together while she was in high school and then occasionally during the college years. She was a lovely kid, but I've known guys who jumped ship rather than put up with the mother-daughter squabbling.

—Jack, 65, lawyer

Another common problem is finding room for the stepparent in the existing parent-child relationship. When a family breaks up and there is no second adult, the divorced or widowed parent may use the child to meet his or her needs for intimacy and become over-connected to the child, particularly one of the opposite sex. If the dad left the household, mother and son may interact in a kind of pseudo-marriage. In the absence of a spouse, a man may come to depend on his daughter as his emotional wife. A parent in such a situation may bond so tightly with the child that there is no room for another person in the family. Coming into this type of situation an adult may feel, as one person described it, "like I'm in a triangle that has only two legs."

In such a relationship, then, the parent's happiness about having a new partner may be tainted by feelings of guilt and betrayal. The parent may feel that the marriage satisfies his or her needs but not the child's and also worries about having less time and energy available for the child. The more demanding the new partner, the more the parent will feel caught between a rock and a hard place. If the situation becomes extremely uncomfortable, the parent will look for a place to put the blame—and most likely it will fall on the new or prospective spouse, not on the child.

From the people we talked to, it became clear that if a second marriage with children is to survive, three things are necessary: The couple must deal with problematic issues before the marriage takes place; they should be willing to go for counseling if any stumbling blocks arise; and they should both be determined to make the marriage work.

Negotiating the merger

The merging of families is a negotiation. When conflicts arise, and they surely will, it will be helpful to put into play one of the most important rules of conflict resolution, which is to break a negotiation down into its many parts. The issues should be addressed as thoroughly as possible, but only one at a time.

But first, there are important practical details.

Does everyone have the same expectations regarding custody?

My husband's ex-wife had the major share of responsibility for their two children both before and after the divorce, when the kids were teenagers. He and I dated for a couple of years, and when we announced we were marrying, she said she wanted the kids to move in with us. She had done her share of child rearing and wanted to build her own career; and she also thought that the kids would benefit from living in a home where there were two adults who had a more regular routine than she [did]. Fortunately, the kids knew and liked me and were already mostly grown, but this change in plans could have thrown a real monkey wrench into our lives. Make sure you know what the plans are before you put your signature on the license.

—Joelle, 56, painter

Where will you live? This is a major concern with school-age children especially. Obviously, your options will be restricted by your budget. If there is a discrepancy between incomes, the family house or even the old neighborhood that the previous spouse could afford may be beyond the new spouse's means. Or the new spouse may be unwilling to move into a residence that the ex had occupied.

One cannot walk into a marriage and take over the empty chair. I didn't want to live with ghosts.

—Eleanor, 65, real estate broker

Yet you may want to keep the children in their present school and are doubtless unwilling to add further disruption to the kids' lives by moving out of a familiar area. Challenges like these call for discussion and compromise.

Instead of deciding between "your place or mine," our solution was to find a home which is "ours." My college-age daughter was enraged at having to leave the old place, but when she realized we weren't about to keep it for her exclusive use, she found an apartment with a room-

mate, then eventually moved back home. It was a way of starting fresh and having our own history.

—Hillary, 51, consultant

Either way there are problems: If the family stays put, the new spouse becomes an interloper and his or her authority may be undermined. If the family moves, the children may resent being uprooted.

One way we overcame our kids' objections was to promise them some things they had been asking for in the new home. One kid wanted a bunk bed, another wanted a four-poster, and all of them wanted a Ping-Pong table and basketball hoop.

—Lynda, 54, therapist

What will the kids call you? Children may not want to use these same titles for stepparents as for their real mothers and fathers. The alternative is using your given name, which may also seem uncomfortable, or a nickname, if that works out. If there will be a mutual child, you may hope that the older kids will call you Mom and Dad so that the baby will follow suit. But such intimacy takes time to build. You may find, if you are living together and not the official stepparent, that you're the "um," as in, "This is my . . . um . . . mom's friend."

When my husband left me, I was grief-stricken, but I didn't want to turn my daughter against her father, so she kept up their relationship. I'd been married to my new husband a few months when he asked her to call him Dad. But my first husband told our child that he didn't want her calling anyone else Daddy. My new husband was insulted and began taking out his unhappiness in small, petty ways. I went to a counselor who told me it was too bad that Tom was putting his feelings ahead of my daughter's because he could make a lot more headway into building a relationship by not putting her in the middle. The counselor said to support her and hope that my husband came to his senses, which, ultimately, he did. But it was awkward at the time.

—Pat, 42, makeup artist

We talked a lot about how we would handle the kids and stepkids. His ex-wife didn't want the kids and couldn't handle them, and he agreed that they would come and live with us—and part of that deal was that they would call me Mom.

—Doris, 43, "domestic goddess"

What surname will the children use? And what name should a woman use when married to a divorcé? Any choice can lead to confusion. If you take your spouse's name and his former wife uses her maiden name in business or reverts to it after the divorce, on occasions like school open-house nights and graduation, people may assume you're the mother of the children from your husband's prior marriage. Or the opposite may happen. If the ex continues to use her married name, then she may be mistaken for the current wife. Another problem that can arise is that sometimes a stepfather is called by the stepchild's surname.

There were so many names on our mailbox, the letter carrier thought we had a commune. My husband and two children used one name; his daughter used her mother's maiden name, which she legally adopted; my children used their father's name; and I used my maiden name. His ex also kept my husband's name, and when mail came for "Mrs. ---," often it was unclear whether it was for me or for her.

—Denise, 48, editor

While none of this confusion is truly serious, it does make for awkward moments. Over time, the issue of who is called what becomes a lot less important.

What duties do you expect one another to take on regarding the children? If you have never been a parent before, you may not fully understand the large amounts of time parenting duties may take. This is a case for full disclosure.

What are the financial arrangements regarding the children? This information has to be put on the table when you become serious about a remarriage. Women who are eager to get a commitment sometimes don't want to "mess up the deal," as one put it, with unpleasant information that might discourage a husband-to-be—for example, the fact that the biological father can't or won't meet his child support obligations.

My stepmother falsely represented her financial situation and my dad had to foot bills that he never expected for her and her four kids that he never expected. He never would have gotten married if he knew the truth because he didn't have that kind of money. The situation caused huge resentment all around, and the marriage was very unhappy.
—Karen, 51, writer

Bringing the children into your relationship

Most people do not seem to spend enough time preparing the children for a remarriage and the many changes that will occur. Once you are in a serious relationship, the prospective stepparents, stepchildren, and step-siblings (if any) should meet. Don't rush into too much togetherness; start with brief, get-acquainted visits in a relaxed, casual setting before you plan any significant time together, such as a weekend. Give everyone time to get acquainted before you announce any plans to remarry. And when you tell your family about your plans, do it in person, and as soon as possible before the projected wedding date to let them get used to the idea.

The husband of one remarried couple made a point of including the children in the process.

I drove my girlfriend and her three teenage daughters to the beach, then walked the girls to the water's edge, asking them to stay about twenty-five yards apart. First I asked the 19-year-old's permission to ask her mother to marry me. "You damn well better," she said. I gave her a rose from a box that I was carrying and told her to keep looking out at the ocean, not at her mother. Next, I asked the 17-year-old, who said it would be cool, and I gave her a rose, too. Finally I asked the 15-year-old, who began to cry from happiness. "Yes, please," she said. Then I went to Cheryl, who was totally mystified, handed her the dozen roses remaining in the box, got down on one knee, and proposed.

—Bob, 61, investor

Though this story ended positively, the fact is that children of divorce, regardless of their age, almost always cling to the magical hope that their parents will reunite, and, therefore may have trouble accepting anyone whose presence will necessarily put an end to this fantasy. They need time to accept the fact that there is a new reality. If the news is sprung on them, it will be more painful, and the children may turn that pain into anger against the stepparent.

We were dating for four years and living together for one, so I thought my stepkids, who were 8 and 14, would figure out that we would get married sooner or later. Finally, we went off for the weekend and eloped, then told the children upon our return. That was ten years ago. Just last month, they told us they were still angry.

—Sam, 46, salesman

The first time I met my stepdaughter, she'd been out of the country for a year. My husband said he wanted to tell her of our plans in person. We picked her up at the airport and, by way of introduction, he said,

"This is Kate. We're getting married in two weeks." I guess it's no surprise she never embraced me.

—Kate, 51, actress

After all, while parents can choose to live with one another, children aren't part of the decision-making process. Moreover, they may well be facing a number of upheavals: changing schools, sharing quarters with new "sisters" and "brothers," and living in a household dominated by a stranger. Naturally, they can feel grief, anger, and guilt.

We had a small wedding when we remarried—just the kids, some relatives, and a few close friends. Four of the five kids fell apart so completely we had to delay cutting the cake for forty-five minutes. My twelve-year-old said, "Now I really know you and Dad won't ever get back together. I love your new husband and I don't even want you and Dad together. It's just a stupid fantasy, but I can't stop crying."

—Karen, 51, writer

Reactions of the former spouse

News that an ex-spouse will remarry often ushers in a new period of mourning. Hearing that a former husband or wife has found a permanent relationship may make the ex feel sad and excluded, since the family seems to be continuing on so well without his or her presence. The ex may also be concerned by the prospect of being replaced in the children's affections by a stepparent. Uncertain of just how to react, probably feeling depressed or isolated, the former spouse may retreat or become hostile.

When I remarried, my ex-husband, who had previously been cooperative, became very petty in his dealings with me over child support. He wrote the checks out to me in my former name even though he knows it caused some confusion at the bank since I had begun to use my present spouse's surname. He expressed to the children the idea that he was being taken advantage of. And while he had formerly been very cooperative in helping out with the kids, he started doing just the minimum required, which made me lash out at him. I tried not to take the bait because I had a feeling that he was just feeling insecure about the fact this was really "The End," and feeling that he was being measured against my new husband. I guess I was right because he sort of got back to normal (as close as he can get, anyway) within a few months and began spending more time with the kids.

—Susan, 39, graphic artist

My second husband was good about making me see how threatened my ex-husband was when I got remarried. Peter suggested that I reassure him that I was very interested in seeing that there were as few changes as possible in the kids' lives and in keeping some kind of emotional consistency—which meant that his being with them was extremely important. I also told him that it was in the interests of the kids for us not to go on the attack with each other.

—Gail, 40, housewife

If necessary, use a counselor or mediator to discuss your concerns and keep the conflicts to a minimum. Children won't adjust to a divorce very well if they are in the middle of a conflict between two angry parents.

Anticipating the kids' concerns

"My mom told us that nothing would change after her remarriage," a 20-year-old college student told us, "and that just wasn't true. I think we should have been better prepared for the life-style changes."

When you tell your children that you are going to remarry, give them a timetable, mention the concerns they may have, what rough spots you anticipate and how you plan to handle them, and then let them have their say. Encourage them to talk about their feelings, expectations, and concerns.

"I think it's helpful for a parent to say 'Relationships are important to me. I believe in marriage, and I want to have one in my life, and I'm choosing this person to be married to. I hope we can get along together as a family,' " says family therapist Audrey Wentworth. That may help a child understand why you are remarrying.

Even young children will understand that something is changing although they can't quite comprehend the change or state precisely how it will occur. Older ones will probably have a great many questions.

Their first thought may be about their relationship with the non-resident biological parent. They need reassurance that that person will remain part of their lives.

Some of their concerns will probably revolve around the new marriage:

- Will it last?
- Will Mom or Dad be happy in this relationship since the other person isn't the same as the previous partner?

Some of their concerns will be about the stepparent:

- Is this new person someone Mom or Dad (and I) can trust?
- What can I expect from this person?
- How does this person expect to be treated?

Some of the questions will have to do with day-to-day concerns:

- Where will we live? Can I have my old room?
- Where will I go to school? Can I see my old friends?

Others will have to do with step-siblings:

• Will I have to share a room?
• How will it be to share my mom or dad with other kids?

You may each have to start by discussing your plans to remarry with your own children alone, and then bring both sets of children together. Airing the issues will provide you with a lot of information about what's on the children's minds and will help you know how the children will fit into your relationship with your new spouse.

A certain amount of anger and resentment is inevitable, along with certain anxieties that are very difficult. You also won't foresee some of the issues that will come out only over time, such as status issues. For example; a youngest child may have to move out of a privileged spot as the "baby" of the family if the merged family contains a younger child. An oldest child may lose seniority to an even older stepbrother or sister. An only child may have to learn to share the attentions of a parent as well as possessions and may also be pressed into taking on responsibilities for new, younger siblings. Other children may be thrust into the unwilling role of caretaker for a new brother or sister, with new obligations and chores.

We injected a little humor into the situation. We told the kids we wanted them to help us figure out where the problems were and we would pay them $2 for a good solution, and $1 for one that would make us laugh.

—Lynda, 54, therapist

"I think that I would tell kids to be accepting of other people," says a college student who has weathered his parent's divorce. "Change doesn't mean something bad; it just means different. Try to look at the changes in your life and your room as something positive, a new beginning with new traditions."

If you both have children

A half-merger, in which only one of the people brings children into the marriage, is difficult enough. In a full merger, with children on both sides, all the problems are magnified.

Many of us grew up watching *The Brady Bunch* on TV. Mike, Carol, and all the children from their prior marriages got along beautifully. But that was a television show. Few people can point out a real-life example of a family that blended as smoothly as the Bradys seemed to.

In part that's because the very notion of a "blended" family is not realistic. If you blend two colors of paint, you get a mixture in which it is no longer possible to distinguish the original independent colors. A family cannot be blended in this sense. You can never merge the original family units so that they are homogenous, with indistinguishable parts. The second family will always be more of a rainbow than a new, mixed color.

It is not unusual to feel that you are part of a tug-of-war.

The greatest sources of stress in our marriage are my husband's children. He is unable to balance things out, gives them whatever they want, and does not consider the effect that has on my feelings and those of my children. Men have a very difficult time balancing the guilt they feel about the previous divorce with the demands of the second marriage.

—Gwen, 48, school administrator

To make the family work, the remarried couple will have to give a lot of thought to establishing common rules, roles, expectations, responsibilities, and goals. Still, the children will have to meet the demands of different systems not only when they move between two separate parental homes, but even within a single home during the times when the parent and stepparent don't agree. Children who become part of a merged family may even decide that *neither* of the two family units suits them, and become totally estranged.

Recognizing the need for help

"A remarriage relationship will face major challenges, such as setting the terms of the stepmothering: how much time is the new wife expected to put in? Thus, premarital and marital counseling is imperative," says Bodner. You and your future spouse might want to see a counselor to prepare for discussions with the children or bring the entire family to see a counselor together. After all, you are dealing with complicated issues for which you are unlikely to be prepared.

"Most of us had no idea of what to expect when we began our journey as a stepfamily," says Robert Klopfer, LCSW. "A lack of understanding of this process and a failure to adjust to it are key elements that cause stepfamilies to fail and couples to redivorce. The stepfamily counselor helps the family develop a map of the territory, a way of finding their unique way to traverse the process of stepfamily development and to find road markers to help the process along. Conflict is more prevalent in early stepfamily life, but it usually calms down when people get to know each other and hopefully, over time, to care for each other."

Starting therapy or marriage counseling early in the process of combining families would help. "When they think about prenuptial planning, most people think only in financial terms. They should do a little psychological preplanning as well," points out psychiatrist Scott Permesly.

You should get joint counseling ahead of time, and I don't mean one or two sessions—[you need to go] enough to bring everything out.
—Bev, 61, nurse

Counseling was a safe place for me to work out my emotional fears and hopes regarding my adjustments to living with a family, with children. I presented it to my husband-to-be as a new experience for us both, and that opened him up to getting help.

—Jackie, 48, criminal defense lawyer

Too few people take that route. They bask in their optimism about the prospects for their remarriage and are unwilling to tackle problems that they hope will never exist.

Even when the adults are willing to see and tackle potential problems, you may find that the children are uncooperative. They may be too shy or too angry to go for help and may need to be coaxed along. Teachers, guidance counselors, and school psychologists, if available, may be supportive and creative in coming up with solutions.

But even if only one partner goes to counseling, everyone may benefit. "If one person in a relationship changes, the other people have to change in response. If I stopped cooking at home, my husband would have to do it or everyone would have to eat out. The point is that if one partner sticks to the counseling, and applies what he or she has learned, the relationship as a whole would change," says Roxanne Permesly.

Another good source for help is stepfamily support groups. They provide an opportunity for everyone in the family—even family members who aren't in residence—to air their feelings and grievances.

Contact the Stepfamily Association of America, 650 J Street, Suite 205, Lincoln NE 68508, or call (800) 735-0329 for information. On the Internet, they're at www.stepfam.org. Also, go to the library and check out all the books that are available. Or go to the bookstore.

I read everything I could on being a stepmom (even though most of it depressed the heck out of me). The reason it helped was that I could see that our problems weren't all my fault. Even though I could not have the "first marriage" picture of my dreams, and even though I truly did not like a lot of my feelings, it helped to learn that they were a normal part of remarriage, especially with nonresident stepdaughters of an unremarried mother.

—Juliet, 47, teacher

Check the Internet too.

The Second Wives Club (www.secondwivesclub.com) has all kinds of support. On message boards people go in and complain about their stepkids, and I get a chance to vent. Remarriage with kids is contradictory: It's hard, but you can also get such joy from the remarriage. Only someone going through it can relate. Parents and friends may be supportive, but you can't really understand what it's like to raise stepchildren unless you are in the same situation. This Internet site is a great sounding board.

—Barb, 45, nurse

The expectations of adult children

It surprises many people to discover that adult children of a prior marriage can become problem factors in a remarriage. But when a parent marries, even years after the children have moved out on their own, any family issues that were unresolved when the children were growing up can resurface. If the children themselves have yet to find a partner, they may even be competitive.

One of my children loved my new husband, but she was having many problems in her own life. She phoned to tell me that she couldn't stand it that her life wasn't working and mine was. Good therapy and the right medication finally helped, but it was difficult for her to see me happy and getting married. We were both in the dating scene at the same time, and in her mind it was a competition of sorts.

—Anne, 63, real estate broker

In addition, adult children may have costly and unanticipated expectations—for example, that a parent will pay for a big wedding, a down payment on a home, or start-up costs for a business.

Dealing with issues that have to do with your children, even when they are adults, is very difficult. His kids like me and vice versa. My husband and I advise each other about most things, but we know what lines not to cross. For example, he is very generous to his kids—great education, big wedding, down payment on the house—but now they're asking us to give them our very expensive car rather than trade it in. I have opinions about that but I'm letting him deal with it.

—Hillary, 51, consultant

In a worst case scenario, an adult child who has failed to become financially independent might expect or need some ongoing support.

Adult children are also very likely to have certain expectations regarding their inheritance, particularly when the remarrying parent has substantial means. The possibility of these prospects changing when the parent remarries may create a lot of anxiety and tension around the new remarriage. The best way to handle this is to let the children know exactly what the plans are.

Before my current husband and I were married, I sat down with his daughter, who is only six years younger than I [am]. I told her I wanted everything out in the open and said she should ask any questions she wanted. She is financially dependent on her father and it came out that she was afraid I would interfere with his support. I assured her that it was none of my business, and that was the end of that.

—Eleanor, 51, columnist

Shortly before my remarriage, and to my absolute astonishment, my daughter asked me if she would be included in my new husband's will! I realized that if she was thinking about that, perhaps his kids were, too. Whether or not they brought it up, they were probably concerned.

I asked my husband to sit down with his kids and tell them that both of us were (fortunately) financially independent, each of us had provided for our own children, and that wouldn't change. Although we had arranged that if one of us outlived the other, money would be available for the survivor, ultimately that money would go to back to the biological children. I think that information made everyone more comfortable all around.

—Marise, 45, art appraiser

Money is not the only issue that may pop up—far from it. Adult children may have very specific opinions about how their parents should behave in every way from where they should live to what standard of living they should maintain. They may simply resent the intrusion of a newcomer, without regard for their parent's need for intellectual and physical companionship.

My husband's ex-wife didn't want him, but she didn't want anyone else to have him either. When we fell in love, she tried to keep the kids turned against him, and they backed her up. I didn't expect her to behave differently, but I was surprised that the kids ultimately seemed more interested in keeping their mother and father involved than in doing what would most promote their father's happiness. It was an unfortunate situation.

—Iris, 61, office manager

Children may also become the self-appointed caretaker of the parent, giving unsolicited advice about the suitability of the prospective partner. They may resent any sign that a new spouse is being treated better than the old one was, and the resultant hostility or criticism will be difficult for a prospective spouse to withstand.

My husband gave me a fur coat, and his son noticed. "I see you have a new fur coat—the first of many, I suppose," he commented. His mother had never had one, and that is a natural jealousy. I didn't wear it around his children, and I just took the remark for what it was. All that's way in the past. We get along very well now.

—Tina, 68, retired

Since children tend to pick up on any doubt you have and use it as ammunition, the best way for you and your spouse to strengthen your remarriage is to be very supportive of one another and to present a united front. The more content you appear to be, the less criticism you'll get. Nevertheless, you may never be able to win the children over completely.

We never had any difficulties in our remarriage because our children were grown and his kids were so grateful and happy that he had met someone close to his age. (He was dating someone way younger when I met him.) But my ex married someone younger than our son and had two kids with her. It's very distressing for my children. They don't know how to relate to their two half-sisters who live out of state. People try to get the children from their first family involved with the second family, and a lot of times those children aren't interested.

—Iris, 61, office manager

If the parents are genuinely committed to the remarriage, and children want to continue the relationship with their parent, they will have little choice but to reconcile themselves to it.

For five years after my husband died, I had been lonely. I expected that might be the way it would be for me forever, but then my neighbor Henry started dropping over for a cup of coffee and a piece of pie each night. I began to feel alive again. When, after a few months, Henry told me how much he cared for me and we began to have a good sexual relationship, I began to feel like a teenager in love. My kids, who were in their forties, were very negative. They seemed shocked that I would consider having a sexual partner other than their dad. They had resigned me to having a celibate life. So I went to a therapist, who told me to write them a letter. I told them that we all loved their dad, and I valued that marriage very much, but that I also loved Henry and he loved me back. I said that I didn't want to be alone, and since Henry had asked me to become engaged, I accepted. I told them that I was having a small dinner party for close friends and family and I wanted them to come and rejoice with us and our new life. If they were too uncomfortable to give us their blessing, I would understand and accept that, though sadly. Fortunately, they came around.

—Alma, 68, office manager

Preparing to be a stepparent

You may not have been wishing to become a mother or father, but if you meet a person with children, they come as part of the deal. They're like the small print in a contract, and who bothers to read the small print? Someone told me that you get what you want by giving someone else what that person wants. That means no one ever gets 100 percent of what he or she wants. It helps to keep that in mind.

—Susan, 39, graphic artist

Don't personalize all the problems. Many people enter a remarriage hoping that it will improve their children's lives. But children typically cling to the hope that their parents will reconcile. How they react to you, the person who stands in the way of their dream, has little to do with you and everything to do with their sense of loss. Not only are they grieving over the loss of the original family, but they are also fearful of a second loss—being replaced by a stepparent in their parent's regard.

Forget your fantasies. A custodial father who is overwhelmed by caring for his children may hope that a stepmother will come in, take over, and re-create a Norman Rockwell family scene. A formerly child-less man may have plans to instill discipline, ambition, a sense of responsibility, or some other desirable quality that seems to be lacking in the stepchildren. A woman who has never been a parent may hope that stepchildren will fill a missing portion of her life by being the loving, responsible children/friends she always wanted. But peaceful coexistence may be all that you can hope for. It's best to keep your expectations low at first, especially if you're coming into a family of teenagers.

Learn to compromise. In a biological family, people develop similar expectations about what's considered normal and acceptable behavior, ranging from manners (Can you leave the table before everyone has eaten? Are hats allowed at the dinner table? Does everyone say grace?) to standards of cleanliness (Can you hang a coat over a chair? Does the bed have to be made every day?). In stepfamilies, there may be serious differences about these issues, as well as about duties and privileges.

We have had only two arguments in twenty-seven years of remarriage, and both times it was about kids. One was that he couldn't understand why my three children called all the time when his four didn't. Men are different from women, I told him. [Women] parent on demand. I told him that even if he didn't understand why the kids were doing what they were doing, he would have to learn to live with it or I would just have to leave.

—Sami, 68, stand-up comedienne

Expect to work hard. Don't underestimate the obligations of parenthood—they're time-consuming and relentless. If the children involved are young, the physical demands can be overwhelming. The days are long, you have no privacy, and the tasks never take a holiday. You're running another whole life (or several other lives), which requires shopping for clothes, making doctor's appointments, going to church and music lessons, planning birthday parties, scheduling vacations, and attending parent-teacher conferences. You may even find yourself wearing a Day-Glo orange vest and circling the block for the after-school safety patrol.

Reach out for help. You may never form the close relationship with your stepchildren that you might like, and you may never like them as much as you might hope. No matter how optimistic and patient you are, this is a difficult situation. If you have never been a parent, you may be shocked to discover how trying, intrusive, and self-absorbed children can be. The most useful strategy is getting professional help and talking as much as you can to other parents, not necessarily stepparents: All parents of teens, for instance, have much to commiserate about.

There will be light at the end of the tunnel! Think back to any new experience that had a significant effect on your life: moving to a new town, starting college, beginning a new job. No matter how positive you felt about these changes, you surely recall moments when you wondered why you were there and if you had made the right choice. Moments like these arise when you're parenting, too, whether the child in question is a stepchild or a biological one. For many people, the first month or two of being a parent is a relentless ordeal of sleep deprivation, chores without end, fears, and anxieties. You second-guess yourself (Am I cut out for this?) and worry endlessly (Why is the baby crying? Is something wrong?). For some parents, bonding doesn't begin until the child sleeps through the night, starts to smile back, and otherwise becomes calmer and more responsive. The process is the same in starting a stepfamily. Though you may be overwhelmed at first, you can make it work. It just takes time.

Interacting with the in-laws

Grandparents may have a hard time welcoming step-grandchildren into the family, putting the stepparent in an awkward situation.

My husband and I have a wonderful relationship with each other and our three boys—my two from a previous marriage and his one. Not only that, but the boys themselves get along beautifully. The only fly in the ointment is my mother. When I refer to my husband's son as her "grand-child," she informs me, "I have only two grandsons."

— Roslyn, 55, book editor

Or the former in-laws may be very critical of the stepparent, a stranger who is helping to raise their grandchildren. But there may be problems even without any children in the picture.

"It is not unusual," says matrimonial lawyer Arthur D. Ginsburg, "for in-laws to have a very strong attachment to the first wife. This makes a situation much tougher for wife number two."

My mother-in-law makes it very clear that she prefers my husband's former spouse. Even though we've been married a couple of years, she hasn't accepted the fact that I'm here to stay. She'll always make comments like, "Rita was so considerate; when I came to visit she always made sure to have the kind of tea I like," or, "Rita kept the house so immaculate, it was a pleasure to see." What I'd like to say is that the reason Rita did such a great job with the housework is that she didn't work outside the home, and I do. In fact, I'm very successful. Fortunately, I know that my husband respects my accomplishments and is thrilled with my achievements. So finally I just decided I wouldn't let her get to me. Whenever she starts talking about something Rita did that was great, I just say, "I'm sure you're right," and move on to something else.

— Elisa, 42, publicist

My husband's first wife didn't work and spent all her time on her appearance, which evidently pleased my mother-in-law. I'm not exactly careless about my appearance but obviously I'm not up to this woman's standards. She actually will say things to me like, "Fix your hair, dear, so you'll look pretty. Harry likes pretty women."

—Roslyn, 55, book editor

When I first got married, I was very young, and I was always trying to please. I used to obsess about his family. "They don't like me; they don't really know me." Then I detached. I'm not negative toward them. I'm nice and cordial, but I don't get involved. I know I'll never have the special place of my husband's ex, whom they met when she was just a teenager.

—Vicki, 40, music teacher

If a woman is remarried to someone who had been a "confirmed bachelor," his family may have trouble with the fact that he now has new priorities.

His family (mother, brother, sister-in-law) was not truly happy when he married at age 42. They liked life as it was and have been a real pain in the neck. Fortunately, my spouse has always backed me up to the hilt, so that I have been able to weather the storms.

—Louise, 60, dietitian

Sometimes in-laws have trouble moving on when their child's marriage comes to an end.

I married a widower a year after his wife passed away, and his former in-laws came to visit. They called me "Little Darling" and my husband "Little Buddy," and they drank too much. It became pretty obvious to me that they had some responsibility for their daughter's drug addiction and death. Fortunately, my husband, who had been a drinker himself, stopped. He became more sane and sober and started seeing them more clearly. More important, once he had sufficient time to properly grieve for his wife, he detached from them—but it took eight years.

—Florence, 43, housewife

Sometimes in-laws don't know how to keep an appropriate distance.

My spouse's extended family was inextricably involved in his life until I became part of it. I was raised to believe that a marriage is sacred and private, but my spouse is accustomed to air marital difficulties among the family. My husband was the baby of the family; he has an easygoing personality, is nonconfrontational, and is basically a pleaser. He has had a fair amount of difficulty adjusting to my need for privacy, because he has allowed his siblings to be very much a part of his life. He's accustomed to getting and taking their advice, and sometimes it's contradictory to mine. That can be a problem.

—June, 37, doctor

Your own attitude has a lot to do with how things work out. It is best if you can start with the assumption that in-laws are nice people who will add to your life in some way; after all, you have in common a high regard for your spouse. They may fulfill your expectations, and you theirs, after a period of adjustment. Besides, eventually their role becomes less important. Try to remember that, and if things are less than perfect, simply bide your time.

"You can't force people to divorce their in-laws," Roxanne Permesly points out. "But over time, these relationships do tend to fade into the background."

Get your spouse's guidance by talking about your feelings and do your best to make things work out so that you don't deprive the spouse of the companionship of his or her family.

My husband's previous wife had no interest in his sisters and parents. They weren't exactly the kind of people I might have sought as friends, but they were generous and kind, so I reached out to them and they have been wonderful to me. Now we spend the holidays together, our only child has cousins he is close to, and my husband is more connected to his family than he was previously. In fact, when we are at family events, I even feel that he feels closer to me.

—Elisa, 42, publicist

Some people work out relationships with their in-laws with surprising sensitivity.

My husband died suddenly when he wasn't quite 30. This was an especially big loss to his mother because he was an only child. We stayed in touch, and when I remarried within a few years, I decided to include her in our family. I made her a sort of honorary grandmother to my children. My second husband was remarkably understanding and cooperative, and I think this is one of the reasons I love and respect him.

—Caroline, 55, university professor

My husband's former mother-in-law is very fond of him. She was able to appreciate what a wonderful husband he was when her daughter was dying of cancer. They are still the best of friends, and she was gracious and welcoming when he married me. She and I are part of one big extended family, and I think the only thing that disappoints her is that I haven't adopted her late daughter's best friend as my best friend as well.

—Hillary, 51, consultant

Include your friends

Your future spouse's circle of friends are probably an important part of his or her adult history, and your opinions of him or her were no doubt influenced by the sort of people they are. Some of your future spouse's appeal may even have been his or her connection to people you find attractive, interesting, and compatible. However, the two of you may have different needs for privacy and socializing. When you are contemplating remarriage, give some thought to how much companionship you will be expected to tolerate.

My second husband is a charismatic guy who has attracted a huge circle of friends, and we live in a popular resort area that draws many visitors. The first year of our marriage, we had house guests for forty of the first fifty-two weekends. At first it was fun, and I enjoyed being the perfect hostess. But after a while, I started to feel resentful of all the work and of having my privacy invaded. Part of the problem is that I like things just so, whereas my husband is far more casual and doesn't feel obliged to provide fresh linens, stock up on things like bottled water, and plan the dinner menus in advance. Finally we had a talk. This whirlwind of activity around him was one reason I enjoyed being with him, but we had to make some kind of compromise: fewer invitations extended by him and a more laissez-faire *attitude on my part.*

—Kate, 51, actress

But be aware that a person who has been single a long time may be very closely bonded to friends and need time and space dedicated to keeping those friendships alive. As the new spouse, you may be expected to make those friendships a significant part of your life as well.

My husband has ten pals who gather together at least once a month. Some of them are single, and some have wives, but that doesn't matter. No wife could come between their friendships. It's their tradition to get together with each other and their families every year on the Fourth of July weekend. None of them would dream of making other plans.

—Gail, 40, housewife

This situation is a perfect example of understanding the difference between an idea and reality. Right now you may have no problem with the idea of spending every Fourth of July with the same crowd, but the day may come when you want to be with your own family or accept another interesting invitation. If your spouse insists that you go along with his long-standing plan, like it or not, you will feel obligated to comply. You may be able to negotiate some time on your own that weekend. That kind of compromise helps make a marriage work.

Most often, it's the man in a remarriage who resents the amount of time his wife is spending with friends. This may be particularly likely in the wake of a broken marriage, when a man tends to be especially isolated. His ex-wife's friends and children will probably rally around her, and since his former wife probably made the social plans, he may now be completely excluded by his onetime social circle. Eventually, when the remarried couple forms a social network of their own, this problem should subside.

Other obligations

If you have any family obligations, like an elderly parent who may expect to come and live with you, be sure to discuss the situation with your spouse before the marriage. And be prepared for the fact that your future spouse may have to meet similar obligations, since people in a remarriage are more likely to have elderly parents. These situations can put a great burden on your relationship.

The greatest source of stress in our marriage was having to leave my wife twice for extended periods to live with my mother when she was in need of intensive care. Fortunately, my wife and she liked one another, and my wife was very understanding.

—Bob, 61, investor

As you anticipate remarriage

You have to check out everything else, but you need a high pitter-patter content [in your heart].

—Karl, 58, inventor

However logically you approach a remarriage—carefully assessing your compatibility and expectations and considering whether you are up to the demands the relationship will entail—two things are certain. What will ultimately persuade you whether or not to go ahead will be your response when you ask yourself, "Do I love this person? Can I imagine us growing old together?" You'll only know if you made the right decision by playing your hunch.

Part Two

MAKING THE
REMARRIAGE A SUCCESS

 *5*

LOVE AND MONEY

Settle as many issues as you can before you get married. It's easier to separate an egg before you scramble it.

—Anonymous

When you fall in love, your focus is primarily on the emotional aspect of your relationship. But once you say "I do" you have made a financial commitment as well as a romantic one. Money and marriage have always been linked and, historically, economic reasons were behind most marriages.

In a first marriage both partners usually start off on a more or less equal footing, but in a remarriage the circumstances may be much more complicated. Even if your financial styles are similar, the circumstances of the remarriage may change your economic situation dramatically. An independent woman who has achieved economic success and is accustomed to spending her money freely may suddenly become part of a union that is encumbered by financial obligations to a former spouse and children from a prior marriage. A man who has been comfortably able to provide for his first family may be financially stressed when he commits what some people call "economic polygamy": remarriage to a woman who needs his help in providing for children of her own. And even if there are no children, a man and woman may come to a remarriage with discrepancies in financial lifestyles which require some adjustment.

In the eyes of the law, marriage is an economic partnership and once you've signed a marriage contract, you are in effect going into business with your new spouse. As with any type of partnership, there is ongoing negotiation and the hope that both people will prosper. Few people would dream of entering a business partnership without discussing all the rights and obligations of both parties, yet people are rarely equally thorough in laying out the terms for their marriage. If the financial aspects of a marriage are not clear a couple may experience problems that are as destructive as those in a troubled business partnership.

Although you might expect that arguments about money are more frequent in households at the lower end of the socioeconomic scale, in fact the opposite is true. The less you have to spend, the fewer the opportunities for disagreement. When a couple is scrambling just to pay the basic bills, they don't quarrel about who pays for which children to go on vacation or why only two of the four can go to summer camp. But once you have discretionary income and there are opportunities for choice, opposing points of view may surface.

Every marriage expert advises couples to have frank discussions about money before signing the marriage license, yet this advice is often ignored. If couples were more forthright about their financial needs before they married, they would find it easier to solve the economic problems in the marriage—or agree not to get married in the first place. One financial analyst estimates that over one-fourth of spouses do not know how much money the other makes. In 1999,

Citibank did a survey which indicated that 57 percent of divorces are about money. Though many people feel awkward discussing the subject of money, once the terms are negotiated, it is usually relatively easy to live peacefully within them.

Financial expectations in a first marriage

People in first marriages tend to be more trusting, less cautious, and more willing to pool their assets. In most cases they have few if any assets to protect and they're less concerned about a potential spouse's financial prospects. With youth comes the confidence that all things are possible. They know a professional has a fairly certain future but may be equally optimistic that a less conventional career will also lead to prosperity; they may be as willing to marry a would-be actor as a law student. Moreover, they don't have pressing concerns about security. What twentysomething thinks seriously about retirement?

Many families today have a standard of living that requires two incomes, and it's usual for a young woman to expect to have a career. But tradition often prevails in first marriages. Men customarily expect to be the chief providers and are therefore much less likely than women to be concerned about the future earning power of a spouse. Responding to a questionnaire for Susan Kelley's book *Why Men Commit,* 100 percent of the men interviewed said it was not an issue in their first marriages whether or not the woman had money. Not unexpectedly, nearly 100 percent of this group also indicated that they did not anticipate problems revolving around money.

Economic concerns in a remarriage

Again, the women in our survey were, on average, 23 years old at their first marriage, and remained in that marriage seventeen years; the men were nearly 27 and remained in the marriage an average of almost thirteen years. So both partners were likely to be over 40 at the time of a remarriage.

At age 40, most of your habits—including your spending habits—are ingrained. And both of you are likely to give serious thought as to what the other person will bring to the table in terms of assets and/or earning power. If money became an issue in the course of the first marriage, those concerns will be heightened.

I didn't expect my wife to work in my first marriage; times were different. But over the years I felt burdened by having all the financial responsibility, particularly because my wife was a big spender. I wasn't going to be burned again. I wouldn't date anyone who didn't work, who didn't know how hard it was to make a buck.

—Phil, 62, sales

This time around, I was looking for a copilot, not a passenger. I wanted a more balanced situation. I got tired of paying all the bills myself.

—Bill, 47, foreign trader

Women, too, bring negative financial experiences to a second marriage.

When I married at 23, I had a good career, money in the bank, and even a stock portfolio. After two babies and five years of a miserable marriage, I walked out. My husband cleared out the bank account and took the stock, leaving me penniless with 2- and 3-year-olds. He was so vindictive he even took refunds from their nursery schools. For a while I was on food stamps and welfare. Fifteen years later, I had rebuilt my career and my bank account, and when I finally did remarry, I knew that in this relationship I had a responsible partner. I would never again give up my earning capacity; nor would I ever dream of marrying someone with a lower economic standard than mine. Maybe that sounds callous, but I learned the hard way.

—Kate, 51, actress

One of the men we surveyed was very articulate in explaining how his prospective wife's financial independence was a big factor in his decision to remarry.

I have to tell you, one of the really compelling reasons that made me marry this woman is that she didn't seem to need one damn thing from me. She'd run her own life and done it well. With a lot of women, I had the sense there was something missing, they were seeking a companion for the security, they were thinking to themselves, If only I had had a rich husband, an earner, then I would have no money problems. There wasn't any of that going on here. It was her choice to be with me.

—Robert, 59, businessman

Many a woman has made a big personal transition between her marriages, and gone from a dependent relationship into an independent one. Whether or not she originally planned to have a career, she may have had to find a way to support herself and, in some cases, her family. The knowledge that she has financial independence affects her self-confidence and feelings of independence. She knows that if for some reason this remarriage doesn't work out, she can take care of herself. But she also knows that some of the petty irritations about money that may have existed in a prior marriage simply won't happen this time around. If there is something she wants, she can buy it for herself.

Financial planning before a remarriage

While earning capacity may have changed, a more significant difference between a remarriage and a first marriage is that over the intervening years, either or both parties may have acquired assets that they are concerned about protecting.

Furthermore, either may have a complex set of financial obligations that didn't exist at the time of a previous marriage: the responsibility to provide total or partial support to ex-spouses, children, and/or parents, along with possible responsibilities to business partners. In addition, there may be unexpected consequences when the remarriage puts you in different economic circumstances.

My children, who were in college, became ineligible for financial aid when I married my husband, and this caused many unforeseen problems. He didn't feel he should be responsible for tuitions of grown children he had never known.

—Kathryn, 48, public relations executive

If a man and woman are thinking about retirement, they may have concerns about supporting themselves in their later years.

We thought about the fact that if one of us became ill, the other person might have to become a caretaker and stop working. This would reduce the amount of the pension that one of us might have to look forward to. That was a concern I certainly didn't have the first time I married.

—Clara, 54, university administrator

And finally, as one of the people we surveyed pointed out, "As you get older, you want more!" In a remarriage, you probably don't have the patience or flexibility to live as thriftily as you did when you were very young, and you may not have ten, twenty, or thirty years to wait for the pleasures money can buy.

In many cases, the economic circumstances in a second marriage are challenging because a single paycheck has to cover the cost of two households. That sort of situation can be a very big strain on a re-marriage.

However, the people we talked to painted a generally rosy economic picture. Among the reasons given that this marriage was happier than the previous one, 42 percent of the women and 41 percent of the men cited an improved financial situation—though 31 percent of the men cited financial pressure as their biggest source of stress.

The need to clarify expectations

A remarriage operates most effectively when both members are clear about who will contribute what to their joint finances. Family consultant Judith Peck, who specializes in couples work with an emphasis on financial matters, says, "Money pushes so many buttons because it is a metaphor for other things. It can be used to make you feel dependent or independent, loved and taken care of or cheated and insecure. But in reality, money is a commodity. A lot of what I do is try to help people disentangle their emotions from the reality of what money represents to them."

"There are two kinds of issues. Women, in particular, often need to be pushed to an adult position where they take responsibility for planning ahead. Both men and women have to learn that 'negotiating' isn't a dirty word. It's a way to develop a strategy. Eventually, all my patients come to understand why these issues have to be addressed."

After all, what reasonable person would sign *any* contract without negotiating every point? There are many issues to be covered for a marriage. Who buys the car and in whose name will the title be held? Who gets the deceased wife's jewelry collection: her children or the second wife? Will your stepdaughter's trip to Europe be paid for with money that's already been put aside or does it come out of the new communal pot? What exactly are the obligations to a former spouse, to your own children, and to your spouse's children? Many arguments begin because the current wife feels her husband is being more generous to his ex-wife and children of a prior marriage than he is to her or her children. Of course, it is difficult to watch family members from a previous marriage enjoying expensive clothes, nice trips, or other indulgences that you and your children do not have. Naturally you want nice things too, but there are more subtle issues at play.

The connection between money and worth

Psychologist Ruth Durschlag says that when a woman looks at how her husband is treating his ex-spouse and the children they had together, she is really wondering, "Am I as important as your former wife?" and asking, "How committed are you to our relationship?"

Many people are afraid that bringing up money matters before a marriage may make them appear needy, greedy, and/or paranoid, and, at worst, create such negative feelings that the marriage plans might be put at risk. Is that possible? Of course. But is it likely? No. Besides, if the prospect of a candid conversation about any sensitive topic makes you extremely anxious, what does that reveal about the prospects for the marriage itself? If you can't manage to get through such a vital discussion, can you make it through a lifetime? Talking about money won't break up a solid relationship; in fact, hammering away at money issues until both partners are comfortable and there is little chance of future misunderstanding should make the relationship more sound. It's probably easier to work out the details of your arrangement while you're both in the infatuation stage and especially eager to please one another.

In many instances of happily remarried people, at least one of the spouses-to-be had volunteered information about financial concerns and intentions before it was requested.

When we got together, he said, "What I have is yours." And I said the same to him. When child support didn't come from my ex, my second husband took on the responsibility of educating my kids.

—Lauren, 55, human resources director

Support was a big consideration. My ex and I had been in business together, and when we split, I no longer had a husband and I also no longer had a job. My second husband knew exactly what the situation was and was terrific about taking on me and my child.

—Lisa, 41, real estate broker

It was very difficult for me to bring up finances. I couldn't even approach it. But my husband brought it up. He was extremely open and aware of my concerns. I was entitled to a pension from my first husband (who had died), and he knew that if I remarried, I would lose it. He said, "You'll be far better off marrying me, so don't worry about giving up that pension." That was not said to entice me, but to reassure me. Very early on, he told me what he earned, what would happen if he passed away, and what I would be entitled to. He wanted to make sure that his children would get something but also that I would be taken care of.

—Miriam, 63, nurse

He didn't ask how much I was making. His position was basically that what was his was mine, and what was mine was mine. He had spent many years alone, and money wasn't important to him. Also, he didn't think I was a "taker," and he saw that I worked and was committed to working.

—Haley, 54, headhunter

Resolving the issues

However unromantic you may find the prospect of sitting down with paper and a calculator, it's how you'll avoid the future problems that unresolved issues and unexpected obligations can lead to. If a son or daughter makes a father feel guilty enough, he may forget that he once vowed to the child and his new wife that he would never, ever pay for graduate school for that child because it would put such a strain on his finances. Or, if your child asks for a fancy wedding, it's tempting to resent the fact that your second husband won't volunteer to contribute to it, even if you swore you would never ask him to supplement the costs of supporting your child. The idea is to have everything spelled out, so there aren't any simmering resentments or fuzzy areas. Financial problems may not torpedo your wedding plans, but unpleasant surprises after the marriage can seriously undermine trust. Consider it a "deal-breaker" if your partner tells you his or her finances are none of your business or if you catch him or her in a lie about personal assets or debts.

Be sure to discuss:

- What are both partners' assets? Consider home, investments, and other valuables.
- What are your liabilities? What does it cost to carry the home mortgage? What obligations exist for child support, alimony, or the care of aging parents? What kind of debt do you each carry? (You should see one another's credit card reports.)
- What kind of budget are you going to live on? Discuss specific ideas for major purchases and long-term planning. What are your spending styles? How much is each of you willing to do without now in order to have more in the future?
- What impact will marriage have on your taxes? Do either of you have any pre-marriage tax debt? Will the custodial or noncustodial parent get the tax breaks? Will you be able to take advantage of any tax breaks if a house will be sold?

How the money situation may evolve

Sharing money is a sign of trust. In a second marriage, you may not be able or willing to intermingle your funds at first. But over time, you should, to some degree, as a vote of confidence that the marriage is working and you believe it will endure. In happy remarriages, this is exactly what happens. Money becomes less of an issue. Partners are less inclined to distinguish "what's mine" from "what's ours."

And as we've said, although traditionally it was the man who brought the financial substance to a relationship, it's increasingly common for women to be the ones who contribute the lion's share to the pot.

I was making more money than my second husband, I owned the house we moved into, and I made it absolutely clear that I wasn't going to be party to his past obligations—which included big debts incurred by his first wife. However, I eventually helped him pay them off. I would like to tell you I was a good sport about it but, in truth, I wasn't. Still, it was the right choice. The burden is behind us, his business is better than it's ever been, and we're in great shape in every respect.

—Rosalind, 48, court reporter

My husband does not feel his children are my financial responsibility, but if I didn't help, who would? My husband is a wonderful man, and I help to take the burden off of him.

—Annette, 48, health care professional

He earned a good living but had no savings. He was going to pay the expenses and I bought the apartment, which meant I tied up a lot of money in my name. I was nervous. I would think, What if I had to support him? What if he's ill and I'm draining all my money? As a result, I kept everything separate. But as time has gone by and the commitment has become deeper, I have become more secure and I have become more and more generous.

—Marion, 50, producer

How a "prenup" can help

A prenuptial agreement is a contract that defines how assets will be controlled once a couple is married. Generally, a prenuptial agreement is drawn up when there is a great discrepancy between the assets of the spouses-to-be. It is more common in a remarriage. In a first marriage, a prenup is usually unnecessary unless one of the people involved has made or inherited a great deal of money before the marriage or expects a substantial inheritance.

In a remarriage, whoever has the larger amount of assets will usually want the protection of a prenup to limit the amount that the other spouse can walk away with if the marriage should fail. If there are also children and/or a business partner, a prenup is even more vital. In the event of divorce, a well-drawn prenup makes it impossible for the spouse to litigate in order to get a bigger share than was agreed upon. In the event of death, the provisions of the prenuptial agreement supersede anything to which the spouse may be entitled by state law.

Even so, there are some advantages to signing a prenup for the person who has the smaller assets. It does establish a maximum—but it also sets a minimum. If the marriage ends, the less affluent person is assured of the agreed-upon amount without having to give discretion to a judge. It may also be advantageous to sign a prenuptial agreement before a second marriage because you are not well protected under the law. Courts have taken the position that a first family takes priority over subsequent ones. Children of a first marriage can get a court order demanding that a father pay for college costs, but the second set of children gets only the leftovers. At least a prenup provides some financial assurance.

However, the point of a marriage is to form a single, sharing entity—to merge two into one. Prenuptial agreements seem to work contrary to this notion because they perpetuate the imbalances. Though it can be viewed as an acknowledgment of reality, the less well-off spouse may interpret the prenup as revealing a lack of trust. Sometimes people agree to sign one and then back out at the last minute. They understand the purpose of the agreement, but the spirit of it upsets them. The people who have the greater assets may become paranoid in response: If you are marrying me for love, not for my money, why do you have a problem signing this?

It should not be seen as an affront if a spouse-to-be requests a prenup. Everyone knows that marriages can and do fail. If you've been divorced or widowed yourself, you've most likely lived through the consequences that arise from financial uncertainty and should understand that a prenup is simply a wise precaution. Isn't it a little foolhardy to risk losing a large part of your assets to someone whom you may not have known very long? A prenup is simply prudent.

When my husband-to-be proposed a prenup at the advice of his accountant and his attorney—who of course wanted to protect him—I was horrified and hurt at even the suggestion that the marriage wouldn't work out. He asked then for a verbal agreement that each of us owned whatever we had at the time of the marriage, and from that point forth, we'd split everything. Now I've come around to thinking it would have been better to put our arrangement in writing because sometimes issues come up that don't seem to be properly resolved.

—Elisa, 42, publicist

In our case, we both wanted a prenup. He didn't want to get raked over the coals again, and I wanted to make sure that what I had or was likely to have would go to my daughter.

—Maggie, 54, lawyer

A prenup is not a plan for divorce

What most people don't realize is that especially in the context of a second marriage, a prenuptial is not just about what happens if the marriage ends. It is very much about how the marriage should proceed. While a young couple in a first marriage will develop their spending styles together, partners in a remarriage have acquired different patterns that may need some adjustment to work in tandem.

A prenup will also clarify any inaccurate expectations about what resources are coming into this marriage. It forces you to put your financial obligations on the table.

My second-husband-to-be already knew about my plastic surgery, I'd told him about the dumb things I did in college (well, some of them), but I was terrified to reveal some of the intimate financial details of my life, like the fact that my ex-husband doesn't always send the child-support payments and that I thought my mom might have to move in with me at some point in the future. My accountant forced us to deal with this in doing the prenup.

—Gail, 40, housewife

Your future spouse may have some undisclosed details up his or her own sleeve. Perhaps your stepchildren have been told that they will ultimately inherit the house that you two are about to move into; there may be obligations to a business partner that would affect your future spouse's income; or he or she may have set plans in motion to retire at a particular age, even if that will require cutting back on pleasurable aspects of the present life-style.

When the relationship is honest, coming clean financially shouldn't be a problem. Sometimes a woman finds it romantic when the man she is planning to marry (and who seems to be well-off) says he doesn't want a prenup. She interprets that as generosity, that he believes the marriage will work out and has no plans to limit what she gets if it doesn't. But his decision could also indicate that he has less money than she thinks or that his funds are all tied up in, and limited by, a trust.

You may not want to sit down and crunch numbers with your romantic partner. You can leave most of the work to your respective lawyers. Just be sure that you and your lawyers are in agreement about what is to be negotiated. And be sure to read the agreement before you sign it and raise any questions you have.

Practical matters that a prenup can address

A prenuptial agreement can spell out arrangements for all of the following areas and can serve as a working plan for dealing with the financial issues that naturally arise in the course of a marriage, including how you will divide your financial obligations. Only the last couple of points have to do with a dissolution of the marriage.

1. Disclosure of all assets: cash, securities, real estate, business partnerships, etc.

2. Disclosure of all liabilities including all obligations, debts, and oral and written promises to children, prior spouses, other dependents. Although you personally might not want to ask for a future spouse's credit rating, a lawyer would have no such reservations.

3. Plans for consolidation. Concerning the personal residence, cars, furniture, and so on, what will be given away, what will be sold, and what will be jointly owned? Who pays for insurance?

4. Plans for retirement. What's in the pension? Who is the beneficiary? When do the parties expect to retire and on what funds will they manage?

5. Plans for day-to-day procedures: How will expenses be divided?

What will be the procedures for paying bills? Who will hold which credit cards? Etc.

6. Provisions in the event of death. Is there any expectation of rewriting wills, living wills and health proxy, and/or trusts? How will property be divided in the event of death? Who is the beneficiary of existing life insurance policies? Will new ones be purchased?

7. Provisions in the event of divorce: Will there be alimony? Who will pay the legal fees? Who stays in the house? Is there a step-up deal written into it? (A step-up deal specifies that the longer the marriage lasts, the larger the divorce settlement will be. Unfortunately, such a deal can hasten the split-up of a rocky marriage. It was reported that Marla Maples had a step-up deal and, as the marriage headed into its fifth year—at which point her settlement would have increased—Donald Trump pulled the plug).

Don't leave it to your lawyers to think through all the financial decisions. Without your input, they may be more or less aggressive than you would like. Try to be logical and realistic, and bear in mind that you are making a long-term commitment. Sometimes spouses complain that a partner who seemed to be content with the terms of a prenup suddenly "flipped the switch" and became resentful after the ceremony took place. That may happen if you take the head-in-the-sand position: Sign now, worry later. If you discover afterward that you've agreed to something that makes you uncomfortable, chances are you will become more and more resentful over time.

For example, if you know that the house you live in will ultimately become the property of your spouse's children, you may be hesitant or begrudging about spending money on it, even if the money is spent to make it comfortable for your use. One solution is to negotiate as part of the prenup for a certain amount of money to be paid to you over the years to compensate for any such improvements.

A prenup may be challenged in court if it can be proved that both parties didn't have representation, if the deal was unfairly stacked in one party's favor, if one partner misrepresented the facts, or if the agreement was signed under duress (for example, if someone threatened at the last minute to call off the marriage unless it was signed). But fighting to declare a prenup invalid is a last-ditch solution. Don't let it happen to you.

Changing the terms

If there is no agreement in place prior to the marriage, a postnuptial agreement can be drawn up.

Going into the marriage, I wasn't about to push for a prenup. But over the years, we have had disagreements about what, in fact, we had negotiated. Finally, we decided it made sense to spell everything out in a written agreement. It was a little uncomfortable working things out, but afterward I think we were both very relieved. We're certainly quarreling less.
—Cyndi, 55, publicist

It is also possible to rewrite a prenuptial. As partners become more sure of one another in a good marriage, their attitude toward money usually changes.

My husband was not very trusting of women, because of the relationship he had [had] with his first wife. When we set up the prenuptial, basically it was to protect him. We used to have a he pays/she pays kind of situation, but now we really share, and I expect him to get rid of the prenup soon. I think in a marriage there's movement. As you become close and connected, I think you look at the prenup and say, "This is a good marriage and I don't need to be protected anymore."
—Lauren, 55, human resources director

When we did the prenup, he insisted that a certain portion of his estate go to his children. If I hadn't agreed, there would have been no marriage. But as his kids went off to have lives of their own and our relationship grew, he felt differently. We have redone the prenuptial three times now, each time improving my position.

—Patrice, 67, librarian

In my case, I was the one with the money. In fact, new financial planners recently helped me to make an allocation for him in my will and they proposed that I arrange it so that he can't have any of my money if he remarries. They called it the "bimbo" clause. I said, "No, don't put strings on it"; I wanted him to have it. That was a big switch for me. When we first married, and the advisors first suggested I leave him money, I said, "Leave money for him to give to a second wife? For him to go and be happy? Forget it." But now I've changed.

—Marion, 50, producer

Instead of leaving it to chance that the agreement will be rewritten, you can put a "sunset clause" into the prenuptial that says that the agreement will terminate after a certain number of years.

Working out your budget

If you do not have a prenuptial agreement, or if the one you have does not spell out how you'll handle day-to-day expenses, you should sit down and discuss each partner's responsibilities before you get remarried.

Your respective premarital behavior may lead you or your future spouse to have inappropriate expectations. How you handle money during courtship may, or may not, indicate how you will deal with it afterward. If a man seems content to only be earning a modest living before he gets married, it is unreasonable for his prospective wife to assume he will suddenly start looking for a better-paying job once the marriage is a "done deal."

Similarly, a man who proposes to a successful career woman probably expects that she will continue to work after the marriage and not live entirely from his income. If a woman customarily splits the tab on dates, she should not be shocked to discover that her new husband expects her to pay her own way after the marriage.

The notion of supporting someone else's needs takes some getting used to. During our engagement, my first husband, (then 23) casually asked how many pair of pantyhose a week I went through. I told him two, maybe three. He started calculating the annual cost of pantyhose alone and literally panicked: How could he possibly afford to support a wife?! A man who has already been married has usually learned to take in stride the responsibilities of supporting a family. However, he's used to his former wife's spending habits. If she was a spendthrift and you can hold onto a buck, you'll look good. But if she was a penny-pincher and you're not, you've got a problem.

—Rosalind, 48, court reporter

And of course, after a period of independence prior to remarriage, both parties have become accustomed to spending their own money in any way they see fit.

It follows then that both the husband and the wife will have to make some accommodations in order for the money situation to run smoothly. Although sharing expenses with another person may mean fewer outlays, in the case of remarriage, there may be as many as four households operating when there used to be two—which may mean less money is available throughout.

Ways to share the costs

Start by figuring out how much each of you can contribute to your joint living and savings expenses. If there is a disproportion between your two incomes, then you might want to calculate your contributions accordingly.

Most couples maintain a joint pool of money to pay common expenses. Sharing money is another way of acknowledging that you are a pair, and having a joint account forces you to make a formal decision about how much you are each contributing to this marriage and which expenses will be mutual. There's a practical advantage, too: Since a pooled account will contain more money, it may not incur bank fees and may be eligible for free checking. There are two possible systems:

Have a joint checking account for household expenses into which each person contributes equal amounts (or agreed-upon unequal amounts based on the amount of your respective incomes). Or have only a joint savings account, and each be responsible for specific bills from your individual checking accounts. That way, you don't have to rely on one another's ability to keep records.

I believe in sharing. But having a joint account can be sticky: You're relying on each other to keep careful track of the books, which doesn't always work out. Also, I think having individual accounts gives us each a sense of independence.

—Esther, 49, singer

After the mutual bills are paid, if there is any balance, you can each draw a check to use at your own discretion.

The other approach is to deal with discretionary money first. Each person puts aside the money which he or she doesn't want to share into a separate, private account, and then places the remainder into a joint account that determines the family's standard of living.

You can set a maximum that either one spends without a consultation. Among the people we spoke to, this number varied widely.

We decided if something costs over $50, we would discuss [the expenditure] with the other person. That's worked out fine with us.

—Beth, 53, office manager

We discuss in advance any check we plan to write for more than $500; otherwise, we spend whatever we think is necessary.

—Becky, 52, graphic designer

You'll avoid arguments and misunderstandings if you share most decision-making processes. Otherwise, one partner may have all the control and the other no responsibility, which can cause problems on both sides. The weaker partner resents the controlling partner, and the controlling partner resents having the burden of making all the decisions.

Of course, it is helpful when both partners in a remarriage have significant amounts of discretionary funds. Then they can make many of their own spending or investing decisions.

He doesn't especially care about air-conditioning, but I am an allergic person and I'm extremely uncomfortable without it. Rather than have a dispute about whether or not it was necessary, I simply paid to have the house air-conditioned out of my own money. Now both of us are happy.

—Roslyn, 55, book editor

We have an operating account that we both put money into, and we bought our house together. But we don't invest together because we have different philosophies.

—Frank, 59, real estate agent

If you give up earning power

I married Harold when my children were in college and his were out of school and working. I had been the sole supporter of my kids. Harold supported his kids, who lived with their mother. When we relocated, I retired from my teaching job. But even though my kids are grown, I want to slip them a little to help them out, and I know I can't look to Harold for help. I understand, but it makes me angry. Money is freedom, it's power, and, most important, it's independence. If I could give only one piece of advice to a woman about to enter remarriage, I would tell them never to give up earning power unless they have some alternative financial deal in writing.

—Emily, 57, insurance adjuster

The moral of the story is to have your own source of income if at all possible. If you work but don't like your job, change it, or train to do something else. Sometimes one marriage can't accommodate two jobs. If you're giving up a career at your partner's request, you need financial protection (which could be specified in a prenup) and you need to negotiate some rights.

After we married, my husband asked that I give up my job so that I could accompany him on business trips. A footwear manufacturer, he makes long and frequent trips to the Far East and he wanted me with him. He also wanted me to be free to go on vacations. Being together and touring the world was wonderful, but not having my own money made me feel powerless. I felt as if he were the father and I was asking for an allowance. When our MasterCard bill arrived, he questioned every item. Finally, I talked my husband into seeing a counselor, who made him realize the situation he'd put me in. Now he deposits a certain amount into a fund that is mine to spend as I wish, and I have a credit card account in my own name. He has my companionship, but I have my dignity.

—Miranda, 60, housewife

If one partner loses earning capacity

What if the unthinkable happens? If one person is laid off or disabled, the other member of the couple may have to bear the entire burden of financial support.

How would you cope in the case of a serious illness? If you are relatively young, this is unlikely to be an immediate concern. But members of an older couple, even if both are in good health, have to plan for such an eventuality. Would you be expected to care for one another? Are there children nearby who could help? Are you covered by insurance, or have funds been put aside to cover a catastrophic illness or accident? If either of you has had the experience of a devastating illness in a previous marriage, it will be easier to bring this subject up, but it should be discussed in any event.

I was a widower with a young child. My wife and I split the bills as we went along but we didn't have any contingency plans for big expenses. Then I had some back surgery and couldn't work for months. She had to pay all the expenses and I was very uncomfortable. Money was a big issue.

—Larry, 45, contractor

Your prenuptial agreement should provide for a course of action in the event of disability, for which you will be at increased risk as you age. There should be disability insurance in place for either (or both) of you, and you may want to carry supplemental insurance even if a company plan provides some coverage. If coverage is unavailable or unaffordable, you have to seriously plan how you would pay for living expenses if one of you became unable to work.

Taking on the entire financial burden of supporting one household (and possibly two) may be difficult, yet it's not fair for the person who is doing so to usurp all the power. But it can be a natural reaction when someone is under stress or feels "martyred." If you've planned for this possibility in advance, everyone will have greater peace of mind.

Ownership of your home

In a famous Massachusetts case, a divorced man agreed to pay his former spouse alimony, and she took him to court when he failed to make the payments after he lost his job. To satisfy his ex-wife's claim, the court looked to his assets. The man owned his home jointly with his second wife. She had contributed most of the money to buy and improve it, but he had contributed his labor to the house. Ultimately the second wife had this choice: see her husband go to jail for non-payment, or sell (or refinance) the house.

To insulate yourself against past or present debts (for everything from alimony to business difficulties), talk to your lawyer about the best way to own your residence together. There are a number of options.

If you are the sole owner of the residence you will be living in and want to protect it from any future claims against your spouse (or your spouse's claims against you, in the event of divorce), make the issue of ownership clear in the prenup. Then, don't let your spouse contribute either to the costs of the mortgage or to the costs or efforts of remodeling the house, so that the ownership of the house is never in doubt.

Joint tenancy is another way to have some protection.

In our case, I knew that I would want to live in our home even if my husband passed away. We had some discussions and then spoke to our lawyer, who set up a trust so that if I survived, I could live in our home until my death, and only then would his children inherit it. The home had been in their family for generations, so I didn't mind that it would one day be theirs—I just wanted to know that I had a roof over my head during my lifetime.

—Leslie, 46, hairdresser

Planning for retirement

The one matter that a prenuptial agreement can't cover is who will be the beneficiary of a pension plan, since only a spouse or child can be the designee. This piece of business must be taken care of after the marriage takes place.

When, and in what style, you plan to retire should be part of a prenup and must be thought out carefully. Are you planning to live frugally in order to retire sooner? Or are you planning to continue working until you've put aside a particular amount of money? Do you care if your spouse retires and you don't, or vice versa?

The conventional advice is to "max out" contributions to any 401(k)—since tax-exempt money grows faster—and put aside as much remaining money as you can. You should be saving 10 percent of your income in your twenties and thirties, and up to 20 percent in your forties and fifties, depending on what's already put away.

Dealing with life insurance

Anyone who has dependent children or a partner he or she supports financially should have life insurance. In an ideal situation, if the in-sured is a wage earner, the amount of the insurance would be sufficient so that, if invested, it would generate enough interest to replace the lost income. For example, a spouse making $50,000 would ideally have $1,000,000 coverage which, invested at a modest 5 percent return, would produce $50,000. Additional life insurance may be needed to provide the cash to pay off estate taxes. Talk to your accountant to work out what is necessary.

The correct beneficiary should be written into all life insurance policies. Neglecting to change the name after a remarriage is a surprisingly common mistake.

My husband told me that there was plenty of money in the policy to provide for me. There was, but he never got around to changing the beneficiary of the policy, and when he died suddenly of a heart attack, his former wife and children got the money.

—Harriet, 64, housewife

Long-term medical care is another type of insurance to consider. It will help in case you are unwell long enough to exhaust your health benefits. If combining your resources due to your remarriage cuts down on your expenses, allocate the money you are saving to cover long-term health care.

Financial obligations to the children

One of the most difficult situations in remarriage is the economic differences that may exist between the children of remarriage. The "half-merger" union, in which only one partner in the remarriage has children from a previous marriage, and the children are supported by both biological parents, is the best possible situation. But if each spouse has children from a prior marriage the only way to keep the situation free of jealousy, negativity, and competitiveness is if both sets of parents contribute equally to the support of all children.

A painful situation can emerge if a former husband refuses to pay child support and the mother is remarried to a man with children of his own from a previous marriage. If her new husband won't (or can't) assume economic responsibility for his stepchildren, her children's financial circumstances may be completely different from their step-siblings'. If, for example, his children enjoy private schools and camps when hers can't, the mother may well feel torn and resentful, and her children deprived.

The husband may feel resentful in turn. Perhaps he is already living up to major responsibilities, which put a strain on his finances; or his current wife may be making him feel guilty; or he might feel inadequate because he cannot meet the combined total of the demands.

Some of the remarried wife's anger may be redirected at her spouse when it is really meant for her prior husband—for his inability or unwillingness to provide for the children. Even though she knows rationally that few men want to pay for another man's children, she may consider her new husband selfish, or believe that his attitude toward her kids shows a lack of respect for her. It's very hard, in such circumstances, not to resent whatever time he gives his own children—especially if hers are in some way deprived.

I was divorced with an infant when I met my husband, who had two daughters from a previous marriage. We lived together for five years, and when we got married he adopted my son legally. We've been together for twenty-one years now. When we married we had six thousand dollars; now we have millions. Only recently did we get around to estate planning, and it was not pleasant. I discovered that blood is thicker than water. His daughters rarely make a point of visiting my husband, yet he wanted to make sure they got their share, including a lot of things that they're probably not interested in but that my son cares about.

—Rita, 60, interior decorator

In all likelihood, Dad was feeling guilty about not seeing his girls during their childhood, and is belatedly trying to make them "equal" to his adopted son. Had the estate planning been resolved earlier, this situation would probably never have come up.

Still, no matter what the prenuptial agreement stipulates, you can never be completely insulated from a spouse's obligations to support children from his or her former marriage. For instance, even if the husband's income hasn't gone up, an ex-wife may successfully sue for more child support if the court determines that his living expenses have been reduced thanks to the infusion of money from his second wife's income. (A prenuptial agreement not to contribute to one another's child support can't override this because the courts generally favor the welfare of the child.)

Financial self-protection

In the aftermath of a death or divorce, many people take a crash course in personal finance. Women in particular may need to learn some of the following lessons.

You should always have some money that you alone control. This is a motivation to learn about investing which should lead you to develop a feeling of independence. Since 90 percent of women end up alone and in charge of their finances, all women should prepare for such an eventuality.

Every individual should build his or her own credit rating. Should your spouse encounter financial difficulty, your credit rating may sustain you both. And if the marriage ends, you will need to use it on your own behalf. To establish credit, get a nationally recognized card (like Visa or MasterCard, not a local store card or gasoline credit card) in your name alone. Build a credit history by using the card to charge, and pay on time.

Money and your sex life

Money is the carrier for a lot of other issues. The connection between money and love has been a theme for everyone from Sigmund Freud to the novelist D. H. Lawrence and many others. If marriage partners are not open and aboveboard about money, their entire relationship will suffer. If one partner withholds actual currency, the other partner may retaliate by withholding emotional currency—sex.

The resentment on the part of the person who is feeling deprived accumulates, and the balance of the relationship is thrown off. What results is a power game with infinite variations. A lot of this has to do with perception, and some of it has to do with reality. Is one partner really asking for too much, and is the other being miserly? Someone can claim that the money is needed for a particular reason (for example, the upkeep of a child or investment in the future) and, on the face of it, the claim may seem reasonable; but, in fact, what's really going on may be withholding.

Whenever one person holds the purse strings, the people in the couple are not functioning as equals. Being in charge of the money can make one person feel valuable, while the other person feels as if the contributions he or she is making are worthless.

Even more subtly, the partner who has the financial control serves as the relationship's grown-up, while the other partner is the child. A parent-child relationship cannot be a sexual one.

Some people's desire for control is so great that they actually choose it over a sex life. You often see this when an older person picks a mate who is willing—at least at the beginning—to be a sort of junior partner.

You will have a better, deeper partnership if you share the financial responsibilities, and if you both know where your assets are, how your money is being spent, and how it is being invested. Being aware of each other's expectations and attitudes and establishing an ongoing pattern of open and candid discussions about finance goes a long way toward making your remarriage strong.

6

THE HEX OF THE EX

There are no ex-wives—only more wives.

—Willie Nelson, songwriter

We were surprised to discover that, overall, the biggest recurring problem in a remarriage is not stepchildren or money but a former spouse, in most cases the husband's. As one woman bluntly put it:

Biggest stress in this relationship? His ex-wife. Have we overcome it? No; she's still breathing.

—Holly, 33, consultant

Some 37.3 percent of women we surveyed agreed with this assessment, and 15 percent of the men shared their sentiments.

This far eclipsed the number of women who said the biggest issue was stepchildren (21 percent) or problems with money (9.8 percent). And it was the second-most-often mentioned problem for men, 31.3 percent of whom—having to cope with supporting two families—predictably put money at the top of the list.

Though ex-husbands may fail to provide emotional and/or financial support on a regular basis, or worse, fail to provide any at all, complaints about ex-husbands are almost nonexistent, probably because most fade out of the picture. The theme of complaints about ex-wives is just the opposite: They are much too present. Unable to detach from their former husbands for any number of reasons, some become extremely intrusive. In addition, present and former wives often engage in very bitter struggles about parenting the children.

"If the ex-wife has not found happiness, you have a big problem," adds psychiatrist Scott Permesly. "She may be resentful that the second wife has taken her husband and his money—and maybe even benefited from new money that he earned subsequent to the marriage. She sees her replacement with all that she formerly had and possibly more—perhaps a new car, a new house, and so on. Unless the first wife is settled and very secure, she's going to create trouble."

Three's a hostile crowd

My husband is legally divorced from his wife. But they aren't yet emotionally divorced. They're still locking horns. Of course, most people get divorced because they can't get along. So why would you think they'd get along any better afterward?

—Becky, 52, graphic designer

No matter how difficult and protracted the legal dissolution of a marriage may be, the process may still be easier and more conclusive than the dissolution of emotional ties between ex-spouses. Signing divorce papers doesn't end the relationship with an ex, nor will it automatically end even if they can't stand one another. Anger and hostility can keep a relationship going just as effectively as love and affection can. And while the presence of children almost always forces the relationship to continue, an ex-spouse can be an irritant in a remarriage even if there are no children at all—and even after the ex is involved in a new relationship.

My husband walked away from his marriage with a mountain of debt and a large amount of child support. His former wife continually discounts him as a father and me as a mother. She doesn't support any of our efforts. Although she is remarried, she continues to be very bitter.
                                                           —Ivy, 28, housewife

Staying linked by the "ghostly bond"

Sometimes the relationship of former spouses isn't marked by hostility, but by some subtle, ongoing connection. What one wife called the "ghostly bond" creates a kind of ongoing static that interferes with the creation of intimacy and communication in the remarriage relationship. Though people have an infinite capacity for loving relationships with children, friends, or family, there is only room for two people in a truly intimate male-female bonding.

For a marriage to succeed, both husband and wife must focus on the new family and do whatever is possible to reassure one another that each is the other's number one concern. Having to respond to the demands of an ex will diminish the amount of time and energy available to make a 100 percent commitment to the new relationship.

Many people are not aware of how connected they still are to their former spouses, but their present partners are profoundly conscious of the ongoing bond, no matter what form it takes.

When the exes are best friends

If the two partners had a "no-fault" divorce, the attachment between ex-husband and ex-wife can be particularly strong. Being connected to the ex in a very friendly way is often a sign that the marriage was based on familiarity rather than passion. Typically, the couple married at a very young age, and the spouses were like siblings—close and dependable friends whose presence was reassuring and familiar. Even if they were unable to forge a bond as husband and wife, the people in this type of relationship may have a very hard time letting go.

There was no hostility, no rage, not even real incompatibility between us. Our marriage just seemed to fall apart because it lacked excitement. Both of us were feeling, "Is that all there is?" We were buddies but there was no passion, and that didn't seem right. But it was very hard to split up. We had been dating each other since junior high school, had all the same friends, and knew absolutely everything about each other. When the divorce came through, we both cried. It was like letting go of a security blanket. But of course we haven't completely let go. I think we're bound for life.

—Carla, 46, advertising copywriter

By agreeing to stay friends, the divorced couple minimizes their loss. Because they had no pull-out-the-stops battles to work through, they don't have to admit to any unresolved problems. They may be slow to be lulled out of their complacency and to examine the reasons their marriage broke up. They may delay facing their feelings—in fact, they may never get around to doing so. Often, what they are spared in terms of discomfort they pay for in terms of personal growth.

A husband who exits a relationship with a no-fault divorce is especially likely to feel guilty about being in a new relationship, abandoning the children to the custody of the ex-wife and parenting another family. When he expresses these feelings, either in so many words or by being excessively doting to his children from his previous marriage, his new wife may be very resentful toward both him and the children. In turn he'll resent her for being angry at him.

When the ex is dependent

Many women are extremely dependent on their former husbands and unaware of the degree of their dependency.

My spouse's ex does not seem to be able to get over the fact that she is not an integral part of my husband's life now. She manipulates their child incessantly and involves herself with the in-laws. Although re-married, she spends an inordinate amount of time concerned about our lives.

—Iris, 61, office manager

Once divorced, a former wife may seek to maintain the link to her ex in a variety of ways that prove to be very destructive.

She denies him visitation at whim, she kidnapped the children, and she ignores court orders. Nevertheless, she was awarded custody and moved three thousand miles away and still keeps the kids. Her name and issues come up in our daily conversation; it's stressful beyond belief.

—Sunny, 37, housewife

Even more dangerous is fabricating allegations of abuse that may get the police involved.

When he indicated he was ready to seek a divorce, my husband's wife returned to the house she had abandoned to him and the children and demanded to move back in. She created a scene and called 911. When the police arrived, she said he had hit her, which was a lie, and filed an order of protection. The therapist said it was a panicked reaction to the idea that he was really going to abandon her. She wanted to create some kind of connection with him even if it was hostility and anger instead of adoration.

—Cyndi, 55, publicist

We have had constant court battles due to falsely filed charges of lack of support. My husband has been agreeable to her demands, but she continued to harass him. We have even had to file extortion, fraud, and harassment charges against her.

—Elaine, 43, tour guide

Another way of prolonging the connection is to refuse to go to work but expect continued financial support. Less dramatically, but still invasively, a dependent ex will manufacture an endless number of excuses to be in touch.

My husband's ex-wife called him constantly and continued to use him as a confidante when we were living together. It infuriated me that he never told her he was living with another woman. He felt he was protecting her but I think he just wanted to continue being her hero. In fact, I think keeping her in the dark like that was harmful. She kept the illusion that he would some day come back to her and didn't finish her emotional separation. She stopped calling once we got married, but I'm convinced that's only because I told him, "Hey, stop this. I'm your wife now." I think she liked the security of having an ongoing relationship with him. And he was getting some kind of pleasure out of it, too.

—Lori, 30, hospital administrator

Women who employ these tactics are relying on the fact that a man often feels a responsibility to his ex-wife, and they make him complicitous. But his role isn't necessarily entirely passive. Allowing the dependency to continue is actually taking an active role in perpetuating an interrelationship and, in fact, encourages it. If he didn't make a habit of bailing his former spouse out of her problems, she would eventually find other resources or learn to become independent. Some men, however, enjoy the feelings of power and competence they get from being a caretaker without realizing that this involvement is costing more than money. By staying connected with his ex, he may cause problems in his new relationship when his partner becomes resentful and loses trust. Eventually, they will blame each other.

When the ex fans the flames

As annoying as the former spouse can be when he or she remains dependent, the intrusiveness can be even more irksome when it appears to be flirtatious. It's not unusual for a divorced wife and husband to continue to act provocatively toward one another.

I was open to having a relationship with my husband's ex-wife, but over time I really learned to dislike her to the point where my current attitude is, "Don't let that psycho near me." She's been remarried for years, but she and my husband have a kind of flirtation thing going. For example, they were in swimsuits at a family reunion—she still comes to all family events—and he said, "Do I have to take my clothes off for this picture?" and she responded, "Don't bother. I've seen that too many times." She's just too familiar. So I finally said to him, "I'm not going to be made uncomfortable anymore. It's too crowded with two wives. Figure out which one you want at family events." Ultimately, he knew I was right.
—Lois, 41, realtor

My husband's ex is still in love with him, and even her kids say she doesn't want us to be happy. She brings up a lot of incidents about when they were dating, and little intimate moments. She just hasn't gone forward.

—Doris, 43, "domestic goddess"

Dealing with the situation

Sometimes it's hard to win in these situations. Simply telling your partner that the ex is too big a presence may have the least desired effect: Instead of apologizing, your spouse may become angry. A husband who continues to be linked to his ex may complain that you are being unreasonable, petty, or childish when you protest that his relationship with his former wife is excessive or exclusionary. To their new spouses, partners who are unwilling to sever these ties may seem inconsiderate and insensitive.

Rather than abandon the relationship in the face of protests from a new spouse, the divorced couple may remain in contact but do so furtively. They may phone one another only at the office, or they may meet in person on the pretext of discussing a particular problem, and the husband won't report the meeting to his new spouse. Probably this behavior is mostly gamesmanship on the part of the ex—a way of proving that she still has control over a former spouse. And though he would probably deny it, the complicitous husband gets excitement out of engaging in subtly rebellious and clandestine behavior.

If the remarriage partner suspects or finds confirmation of what is going on and accuses the spouse of being insensitive to her feelings and blind to how his ex is manipulating him, he may put forth arguments that at first hearing seemed logical. After all, he and the ex share concerns about the children. They have a history together that he can't simply forget. And he has always helped his ex with her finances, business affairs, and relationships with her family, and he is simply doing the decent thing by continuing to do so.

Or he may simply accuse his new wife of being crazy and insecure. He may express resentment that she needs reassurance and argue that she is trying to control his friendships and his time. This is all deflection and denial. In reality, he's the one with the control issue.

Some women have found creative solutions to the intrusiveness of a spouse.

My husband didn't care that his ex called often, at all hours, but I did. So I asked a friend to start phoning constantly. I pretended it was my former husband, needing to talk to me. After a week, my husband got the message. His ex-wife's calls stopped abruptly.

—Kim, 34, beautician

If calls at home have become annoying, you can also ask that the ex confine the calls to the office, during business hours. But it is your husband's responsibility to mention when such a call has taken place—in fact, it's reasonable for you to expect to be advised whenever a spouse has had contact with the ex and also of any arrangements that affect her and/or the children. Keeping you in the loop is not an issue of control but of courtesy and practicality.

The current wife versus the former wife

"What also may be going on is that a new wife is resentful of the former spouse," says therapist Jill Muir Sukenick. "If her husband is paying alimony or child support, she chafes under the financial burden. Often, too, she feels cheated of the adulation and adoration that was bestowed on the first wife and believes that she's getting the leavings—a more modest apartment, less jewelry, less of whatever a husband might have afforded when not supporting two families.

"One message often replays in the new wife's head—'I'm not her'—even if the husband says, 'I always hated that witch,' " says Sukenick.

"And she hears the same message whenever she's dealing with her stepchildren. It takes a lot of self-esteem and confidence to be able to hold your ground."

Finding some compromise

One of the lessons many people take away from a bad first marriage is how important it is to express your feelings. Sometimes this means drawing a line in the sand at the point where someone else's needs are encroaching on yours. Setting a boundary is not the same as acting defensively. Defensiveness is negative and unyielding; it is characterized by stony silence, enforced civility, combativeness, or defiance. Boundary-setting is an attempt to reach a compromise.

Setting boundaries is often necessary in the complex structure of remarriage, where not just a partner but also kids from prior marriages and aging parents may demand your time and energy. Since these obligations take priority over the needs of an ex-wife, you have to find ways to prevent her influence from spreading, kudzu-like, into your new relationship. This means coming to terms about a variety of issues:

- Whether one spouse is being too controlling or reactive;
- Whether the other spouse is being too accommodating;
- To what degree the demands of the former spouse are, or are not, reasonable;
- How to discourage demands that are excessive.

Both you and your partner must be able to air your feelings about the triangular realtionship without being criticized or shouted down by the other person. You need to assess not only the present situation but also how it is filtered through your individual histories so you can separate what is perceived from what is real. You both need attention, appreciation, and reassurance. The strength of your relationship rests in part on how well things are sorted out and what limits are set.

One wife in a very complicated situation found a gentle way to make her point without anger and hostility.

The ex-wife in my situation is unfortunately very sick right now. She has multiple sclerosis and is a complete invalid. During our courtship I tried to be as understanding of this situation as possible even if it meant our living together while he ate dinner with his ex-wife twice a week. When we got engaged this practice stopped, but he still kept some things in her house, claiming that he didn't have the time to get around to them and didn't have the space for them. Many of her needs were put first. Finally I told him that at 28 years of age I could not marry someone who was partly married to someone else. [I told him,] "I'm sorry that she is sick and I recognize that she is the mother of your child—who is being cared for by me—but I deserve to marry someone who puts me as his first priority." I think the best thing I did at that point was to ask him what advice he would give his daughter if she ever came to him in the situation that I am in. He said right away that he'd tell her to get out of it; he wouldn't want her to be someone's second priority. I just looked at him. Suddenly his entire attitude changed.
—Marlene, 28, teacher

If the husband and wife can't come to some empathic solution, counseling may be necessary.

Money and the ex

"When is the check coming?"; "I need more." Much of the ongoing contact between divorced couples can be reduced to one of those two sentences. Alimony payments are not as common as they used to be, but many husbands have large child support obligations, since an ex-wife often takes the position that her former husband's obligations to their children do not change even if she is remarried to someone who is financially well off. For their part, current wives resent what is often an ongoing financial strain. Some create ways to cope.

I found a really effective way to deal with the stress and agitation around his former wife's constant requests for money. I took over all the finances for our family, and that includes writing all the checks. The wife doesn't like it, but it's cut down on the number of calls asking for money.

—Megan, 31, executive secretary

I couldn't stand seeing those checks to the ex going out of our household account. I just saw it as an invasion of my life. So I asked my husband to set up an entirely separate account so this awareness wasn't constantly in my face.

—Christine, 45, nursing home administrator

If there's enough money involved, another solution might be to hand the responsibilities over to an accountant so as to avoid dealing with them personally.

My feeling is, I don't want to know what he spends on his ex and the kids if I can't change it.

—Vicki, 40, music teacher

Power plays with the children

The most effective and usual way for a former wife to maintain control is by using the children as pawns or acting as if they are agents in enemy territory.

There are times in which I feel that she controls our marriage. In one breath, she will say she is encouraging the girls' relationship with their father, and in the next she tells him they are old enough that, if they don't want to see him, she will not force them to. My husband is a peacekeeper and keeps putting up with her. Many of our plans have been ruined due to her inability to cooperate.

—Penny, 45, child care provider

When her son comes to visit, she talks to my stepson a hundred times a day. He has his own phone at our house, but if I ever pick it up, just trying to be nice, taking a message for him, she gets indignant. "What are you doing on this phone?"

—Roslyn, 55, book editor

My stepson used to be debriefed by his mother after each visit with us. I resented being spied upon.

—Rosalind, 48, court reporter

Coparenting issues can provoke ongoing battles between current and former wives.

The ex doesn't have trouble with me as a new wife but she resents me as a stepmother to her son. She refuses to acknowledge I might have anything of value to say even though I am trained in this area and am a mother myself. She has slandered me, she appears unannounced at our door, she calls our home frequently and pages my spouse relentlessly. She is also very close-mouthed about my stepson's schedule of events when he is with her; yet she becomes enraged when she herself is not filled in on what's happening.

—June, 37, doctor

Sometimes the new spouse finds a solution to the problem.

My husband's ex-wife told me I had no business disciplining her kids— even though they lived with me. Their father was working. Who was supposed to tell them what to do? "I am," she said. I said that was fine, and for the next two weeks I called her at work all day long. I'd say, "Kid Number One is doing such and such; what should I do?" or "Your son wants to go swimming. What should I tell him?" I wasn't being mean or vindictive; I was just tired of fighting. One day, she had a client in her office and she got ticked off. "Stop calling," she said. "Can't you make any decisions?" I reminded her these were her rules: either she let me make the decisions or she would have to. After two weeks, she got tired of all this.

—Doris, 43, "domestic goddess"

In all cases, the best way to approach the problem is to consider the children's needs first.

Staying focused on the kids

Ongoing expressions of hostility will create difficulties in coparenting and take their toll on the kids. For the benefit of the chidren, it's important to learn to let go.

My husband has very little success dealing with his ex-wife. If he goes back to her and tells her to stop doing the things that annoy and hurt me, she takes it out on their son. One day, I showed up at her house to pick up my stepson nine minutes early and she went berserk, calling me names and telling me I would have to wait. She hates when I say that I have three children, a number that includes my stepson. I wish she could just understand that what's important is who you love. I love my stepson, and whatever she does I can live with because I'm the adult and I want the best for him. Years ago, I'd think about her all the time. But as I get older, I find that her anger and abuse just slides off my back. The more active I am and the busier I get, the less time I spend thinking about her.

—Marcy, 37, designer

The first year or two, I was really very angry and hurt because I had worked so hard to make the marriage work. I gave the marriage every-thing and it didn't do any good. I was bitter and upset, and then I saw what those kinds of feelings were doing to other people's children. We decided to put our daughter's needs before all of our own needs and do what was in her best interest, meaning we had to bite our tongues sometimes, and that is what we did. What really helped is that I finally realized that the ex was not going to change and that I had to. I had to let go of the things that were out of my control and just accept her for who and what she is. Since then, our lives have improved 100 percent.

—Doris, 43, "domestic goddess"

"In Florida, prior to getting divorced, everyone with children has to take a four-hour course designed to help you coparent. The mother and father can't attend the same session," says Scott Permesly, the psychiatrist. "You learn about the usefulness of periodic meetings— for example, before summer vacation, or before school begins— which can be used to sort out things like pickups from dance classes and Little League, and so on.

"The new wife has to understand something about the biological mother's power and want her to be happy rather than alienated, and the biological mother should be grateful to have her on the parenting team. Instead of feeling threatened, she should see the new wife as someone who can help her," says Permesly.

If stepparents and former spouses are mature enough to put the interests of the children first, their relationship can be smooth and productive.

My children's stepmother and I get on famously. We both care for and protect the children. I have no fear that my kids will love her more than me or that I will appear to be less in their eyes because of her. I am very confident of my relationship with my children, and I am proud to have raised such generous and loving people. They have accepted their stepmother from the start simply because I did. It is unfortunate that adults become so entangled in what has been "done" to them, and how much they have had to endure, that they totally lose sight of the children.

—Robin, 39, dentist

Family events and the ex

Whether or not the current and former spouses get along, there will be some gatherings to which both might reasonably be invited: major holidays, weddings, graduations, and the like. Some people are able to handle these situations, and others find them uncomfortable . . . or even unbearable.

It's amazing how long it takes people to come to grips and realize that it's over when there's a divorce. When my husband's mother turned 80, his sister invited his ex-wife to the party. I felt it was a discourtesy to me that she was invited when I have let it be known that her presence is uncomfortable for me: The woman has missed no opportunity to make life difficult for me on every occasion when we have been together. So even though I would have liked to be there, we just decided not to go. Fortunately, my husband took a stand with me and set a precedent. We never had the problem again.

—Iris, 61, housewife

When we were first married, I was told that we had to include my husband's ex-wife "for the children's sake." Even kids in their early teens are quite capable of understanding that they should not expect their divorced parents to operate as a family anymore. This may cause them some pain, but it's not right to let them live with a distorted reality. We don't become one big, happy, polygamous family for holidays.

—Rosalind, 48, court reporter

"As a newcomer to the family, you must understand that you can't force people to divorce in-laws. At certain kinds of events such as graduations, marriages, and christenings, naturally both biological parents would be in attendance. But sometimes former wives intrude themselves where they definitely don't belong: they show up in the same resort town on a vacation or go to cocktail parties that they could skip. That's an example of a bad divorce: in other words, there was no emotional separation," says therapist Roxanne Permesly.

The ex's presence can make a second wife feel that her role and status are being undermined. Explain to your spouse that if his prior spouse is to be included in family gatherings, you need to have his family make an effort to help you feel welcome and important. "Your spouse should help draw the boundaries to the children and others, and explain that you are now the main family," Permesly says, "and you should make a point of attending these celebrations to establish yourself as part of it."

When my husband's elder daughter was married, the wedding invitations went out in his and his ex-wife's names only, though both parents had been remarried for many years. I let it go to keep the peace, but when the second daughter got married, I asked that the invitation be extended from "the families of" the bride and groom. It was appropriate and everyone was happy. Check the etiquette books and find out what others have done if you have a similarly delicate situation. Not dealing with it is not the answer. Nor is making too big a deal of it. Some things I just gulped down because it's just one day and it's the bride's day. I try to keep it all in perspective.

—Lois, 41, realtor

Over time, as the bonds strengthen, a spouse usually takes the primary place in the family hierarchy and feels more comfortable assuming that spot.

Gone, but not forgotten

A former spouse does not even have to be actively present in your life to be an intrusive factor.

Once they're out of a bad marriage and no longer irritated by an ex on a daily basis, men in particular may allow their former wife's stock to rise. That's because while the second wife is the one he sleeps with and actually likes, the first wife becomes ennobled as the mother of his child.

Or, a former spouse may not have put closure on the relationship.

I was at my wit's end when I was dating my husband because he talked endlessly about his former wife. It seemed that no matter where we went or what we did, he'd compare our experiences. "When I went skiing with Linda, she said she hated it after a day and I spent the rest of the week on the slopes by myself." "Linda never wanted to go to French restaurants because she said all the food was too rich." It's true that every incident he mentioned was proof once again of what a colossal pill the woman is and, believe me, he knew that was true. So that gave me all the more reason to be resentful of the fact that this awful person was a ubiquitous presence in our lives. Even when we were having a good time, out would pop a reference to Linda. Then I read something by Dr. Joyce Brothers. She said that a person who is recently divorced brings old issues into a new relationship in order to resolve them, and that asking that person to stop doing it might be destructive to the new relationship. The fact that he was willing to share his feelings showed his trust, which was good. However, she did say that it was okay to indicate to him in a sympathetic way that I wanted to concentrate on our ongoing good experiences rather than his past, negative ones.

—Rosalind, 48, court reporter

A friend of mine once told me that your husband's underwear preferences are imprinted by his mother. And I found out that my husband's household habits were all imprinted by his ex-wife. Because she washed all the dishes before she loaded them into the dishwasher, that's what he did. Because she told him you had to carve the leg of lamb horizontally, he criticized me when I did it my way. I guess what really bothered me is not so much the specifics but how my ex was inviting his former spouse into our marriage. I told him that when he did this, it appeared to me he was missing the ex. I told him how I felt and that helped a little. It also helped that over time we built our own store of habits.

—Betty, 45, casting director

If you tend to feel jealous, remind yourself that your present spouse did, after all, leave the ex behind and choose you instead.

You know the gold standard? My husband used his ex-wife, Alice, as the gold standard for beauty. It didn't so much bother me when he looked at beautiful women, but it did bother me whenever he would say, "She looks just like Alice Kelly." The funny part was that he seemed to think they all looked like her, whether they were short or tall, dark or blond, willowy or bodacious. At first this made me very uncomfortable, because I'm not that secure about my looks. Then someone reminded me that if looks were all that mattered, how come so many of People Magazine's *"50 Most Beautiful People" have been divorced? You just have to tell yourself that your spouse moved on to someone he or she liked better—you. If the ex was all that great, the marriage would have stayed intact.*

—Elisa, 42, publicist

A deceased spouse can be an intrusive presence in a remarriage even if that person was not particularly admirable. Our brains are programmed to remember good things and forget bad ones. The widow or widower may recall the former spouse as perfect—and the current spouse may have trouble living up to this idealized specter.

Try for distance and perspective

Decide whether what's bothering you is truly significant. Is it worth fighting over? If you were more secure, would you let it go? Sometimes just saying, "I feel insecure when you . . ." is a way of getting your spouse to respond to you when nagging does not work.

"Be gracious. You can't get into the battle. You've already won the war. You and your spouse have each other," points out Roxanne Permesly.

If I ever meet my ex-husband's wife, I want to shake her hand and thank her for throwing him back in to the marketplace.
                                                    —Debbie, 33, dental assistant

The ex has tried to make our lives sheer hell, but the one thing she can't take away from us has been what brought us together: the love and "oneness."
                                                    —Elaine, 43, tour guide

Remember that time heals

As your relationship with your spouse becomes closer, you may be able to ignore even the most intrusive of ex-wives. As one woman wrote to newspaper columnist Ann Landers, "My husband has three ex-wives and they all call him for one thing or another. It doesn't bother me at all. Being No. 4 is just fine when you know you are No. 1 with your husband. At no time have I felt threatened and my confidence has made our relationship stronger."

Even if you are coparenting, your interaction with your former spouse becomes increasingly minimal.

My ex is very far out of my life now, except for the trickle-down effect he still has on the children. It seems as if I am still expected to put them back together when he fails, over and over again. But he has no effect whatsoever on my current marriage.

—Faye, 45, songwriter

The people we talked to felt that things generally seem to work themselves out.

The biggest stress on our relationship used to be my spouse's ex. We have overcome it. I don't let her rent space in my mind anymore!

—Wanda, 42, business owner

I found it useful to read [Ann Crytser's] The Wife-in-Law Trap. *So little is written about the weird state of dealing with the woman who used to be married to your husband and is still the mother of his children. I was not prepared, and fought being part of what felt like a polygamous relationship. In fact, many of my problems with my stepdaughters stemmed from my intense dislike of their mother, how she behaves, and how much of her I see in them. As I have worked through my feelings about my husband's first wife, my relationship with her children has dramatically improved. I had to process a lot about myself and my feelings about this "other woman" before I really found a lot of peace. I've been at it almost five years and, these days, I'm feeling pretty good about everything.*

—Juliet, 47, teacher

You may even surprise yourself and move beyond tolerance to rapport.

Now I am best friends with his ex-wife. We e-mail each other. We talk about the kids. I can see now why he married her. They were two decent people, too young themselves when they got married. If there was anything I would do differently in my marriage, it would be to have gotten closer to his ex-wife much, much sooner. But jealousy kept us apart. Then, over the years, after births and deaths, you get past those things. Parental warfare is very hard on the kids. They just want love and security. Now we have a seamless family, and it is wonderful.

—Kyla, 47, journalist

REMARRIED . . .
WITH CHILDREN

A dysfunctional family is a family that has more than one person in it.
—Mary Karr

About 65 percent of remarriages involve children from a prior marriage. But when we asked men and women about the greatest source of pleasure in their remarriage, relatively few mentioned children. It can be difficult enough to deal with children who carry one's own genes and with whom there have been years of bonding. It is extraordinarily difficult to deal with someone else's child, even if that child is the offspring of someone you love. The relationship is not 100 percent natural, and the affection is not spontaneous.

Shortly before I became a stepfather, a friend of mine who is a naturalist said, "You know what chimpanzees do when they take a new mate?

They kill the offspring of [their] prior spouse, which makes sense. Why would you want to invest so much time in someone else's genes?"
                                                    —Karl, 58, inventor

"It's a myth that the new husband will take care of your kids," says consultant Judith Peck. "Your children already have a father." And although women are supposed to be the more nurturing sex, not every stepmom feels maternal toward the children of her husband's ex-wife. Yet, as therapist Roxanne Permesly points out, "Fathers don't always understand what the parenting role requires; so the second wife may take on a lot more of the role than she might have expected."

It's no wonder that the hated stepparent is an ancient archetype. Think of Cinderella and her stepmother and Hamlet and his stepfather. At least in the past, you were generally taking over for a parent who had died; today, you're often just a substitute player, subject to scrutiny and criticism not only from the world at large but also from the person for whom you're filling in.

When we asked the people we surveyed if they would remarry, 42 percent of the women and 51 percent of the men said yes, and another 11 percent and 13 percent respectively said yes, but with qualifications—and what they stipulated most frequently was that no children should be involved.

If I had known how difficult it would be, I wonder if I would have chosen to marry at all, or [if I would] at least [have] waited until the children (together we had five, all under ten) were older.
                                    —Eleanor, 65, real estate broker

But when love strikes, many people go ahead and get married despite potential problems. Often they have the fantasy that the remarriage will allow them to create a new and perfect family. They would like their children to be as warmly embraced by the new spouse as they themselves are. The childless stepparent may not only hope to get along with the children but, as we have reported, she or he may also harbor a wish that they will become the loving offspring she or he never had.

We dated for three years to give everyone time to adjust, which they did. But then we were married and a whole new adjustment had to take place.

—Hannah, 34, government worker

No one can foresee what will happen after the remarriage. Even if you have already been living together and learned to accommodate one another as a stepfamily, new problems typically arise after the wedding. It's the turning point when everyone realizes that from this moment on, the arrangements are permanent.

The kids wanted us to get married. They wanted security. But I had to decide that I was ready to take on the real responsibility of the children. As I matured, I realized that once we were married, I couldn't go on treating them as I had been, as if I were their camp counselor, playing with them and going to Chinese meals at midnight on the weekends. Now I had to be a real stepmother who had to deal with the kids' vacations, school, money problems, whatever. And I wasn't sure if I could handle it or even if I wanted to handle it.

—Kyla, 47, journalist

His girls and I all got along great, but now that we're married, they are torn between their mother and me and things aren't going so well.

—Angela, 33, customer service representative

This is a typical scenario, says family therapist Audrey Wentworth. "I knew of a case where the daughters were very happy and accepting; but about two months after the marriage, the stepmother was hearing, 'You can't tell me what to do, you're not my mom'; 'I don't like you.' When she became a stepmother, she had rules. Before that she didn't.

They had to do a lot of problem-solving in family therapy to work it all out."

A mixture of emotions

Love and marriage may go together like a horse and carriage, but love and remarriage aren't as neatly complementary. The carriage may be so crowded that the horse has trouble pulling it.

If you're assuming that the issues involved in creating a stepfamily will be easy or few, you're living in a fantasy. You will not immediately (or, perhaps, ever) love stepchildren as much as you love your own. If you are already a parent, you have learned that bonding isn't always immediate—it takes time, patience, and forbearance—and that there are ages and stages when you find your own kids to be less than lovable; but you are bound to them by history and probably by genes. Nevertheless, even if you never come to love your stepchildren, you may learn to like them.

You'd have to be made of stone if you never took their behavior personally or reacted to ongoing criticism, challenges, or more subtle slights, such as conversation stopping the minute you enter a room.

And there is no way you can ignore the impact of events that took place prior to the remarriage and the feelings they evoked in the children. Even a newborn comes into the world with certain predilections and temperamental quirks, and to that are added an entire history of accumulated experience that can't be forgotten or undone.

The fairy tales that concluded, ". . . and they all lived happily ever after," weren't written about stepfamilies. Constituting a new family out of two that were broken may seem less like the formation of a partnership than the aftermath of a hostile takeover.

"When people come to see me with problems regarding their children, they think the problem is only the children. I always find that the problem is the parental unit," says therapist Joan Soncini.

Putting a lot in, holding a lot back

A stepparent who hasn't had much experience with children may find the amount of time and effort required for child care to be overwhelming. It is normal for children to be annoying, distracting, noisy, and demanding, sometimes all at once, but this will come as a shock to someone whose experience of kids is confined to reminiscences of his or her own youth (back when all children were perfect).

After I got divorced, I had the three kids for weekends only. I'd lived with them, so I thought I knew what would be involved, but I nearly went crazy those first few weekends. I dated a lot of women who had never had kids and told me how they'd love to be a mom to my kids, but I knew I had better marry someone who had been a parent herself so she knew what she was getting into.

—Bill, 47, foreign trader

To keep the peace and—more importantly—keep the marriage healthy, a stepparent may have to put a great deal more into the relationship than he or she ever gets back. You may go to all the games, plan birthday parties, and lend your stepson the car. You may feed the kids good meals when they're with you for the weekend, send them back with clean laundry, and take them on vacation, but don't count on getting thanks from them. And you certainly shouldn't expect thanks from the absent parent.

Always keep in mind how important children are to their parents and how much the parents are bound to them. The children will always be a presence in their lives (if not physically, then emotionally) and will always take precedence over everyone else. You'll get off to a much better start with your stepchildren if you accept these facts.

Remember that you're just the new person marrying into the family. If you don't give more than 50 percent, your stepchildren will be upset—

and so will your spouse. Now that the kids are adults, life is easier. They respect me even though we don't always agree. I don't have a problem with that. They were part of his life for a long time. And I have to say that even with some of the issues we've faced with the kids, this marriage has been a lot easier than my first.

—Fran, 61, saleswoman

Children are often catalysts for the most profound disagreements in a marriage because they become the carriers for so many issues. For example, if your spouse is ignoring your son or daughter, not only will you feel bad for the child but you will probably also wonder what your spouse's behavior says about his feelings for you. After all, if he truly cared for you, it seems like he would care for your child by extension.

Children and their stepparents

It's only natural that children coming to a remarriage will have concerns about a new and changed existence, and they're likely to experience a wide range of negative feelings. Again, remarriage is the ultimate proof of the futility of the dream that children of divorce usually hold—that the family will reconcile: so while the newly wed parents are basking in the glow of a new love, the children may be experiencing feelings of loss, grief, and sadness.

I had to accept that my stepdaughters and I were coming at this marriage from completely different places. In the beginning, the sources of my greatest joys were often their sources of greatest grief. This was not fun for any of us, my husband included.

—Juliet, 47, teacher

My older child and younger one haven't been an issue, but my middle son has had a lot of trouble accepting that things are really over between his father and me. It has taken a lot of communication between my husband and me to deal with his attitude problems.

—Janet, 33, housewife

I hadn't realized how enduring a child's fantasy of reuniting Mom and Dad can be. My husband's girls were in high school when we married, and we've been together fifteen years. Yet when my husband's daughter was married, all the wedding photos she chose to display in her living room featured her mother and father. I'm conveniently out of camera range.

—Lois, 41, realtor

Now that the remarriage has taken place, in a child's mind the parent "belongs" to the new spouse. What's in this for the child? He or she is jealous of the newcomer, who is a constant rival for the parent's love.

Children are also likely to be angry at their parents, both for having split up and for having remarried. Or, being egocentric by nature, they may have concluded that they were responsible in some way for the breakup, and feel guilty as a result. And they are no doubt anxious about what it will be like to live in a stepfamily.

Having lived through a divorce, they may be wary of bonding with a stepparent out of fear that this marriage, too, may end, and another bond will be severed. Often, they feel that any move toward intimacy is an act of disloyalty to the biological parent. This push/pull sensation is a particular problem for young children, because they are forced to be so dependent on a stepparent.

But younger children usually adjust relatively quickly and easily. On the other hand, adolescents, who are notoriously difficult, will probably create most of the problems. They are mature enough to have some real sense of the emotional and psychological issues that surround their change of circumstance. Under the best of circumstances, teenagers are apt to be emotional, uncooperative, contrary, and withdrawn much of the time, so it is pretty much a foregone conclusion that they will be at their worst when their new stepfamily is forming.

My daughter was totally obnoxious. She told me that she thought I could have done much better [than my second husband].
                                        —Lauren, 55, human resources director

Many people are shocked, disappointed, and annoyed when their children misbehave or seem depressed at the very time when they themselves are filled with such enthusiasm and optimism. It is not unusual for both the biological parent and the stepparent to feel they are in a hopeless situation and that, no matter what they do, they won't reach a truce with the stepchildren, and the family will never unite.

Starting off on the right foot

Reassure children that having a good relationship with a stepparent won't endanger their relationship with their biological parent. Above all, don't criticize the other parent. If you respect the fact that children have other allegiances they're less likely to feel conflicted about those relationships.

One of the best ways to bring members of the stepfamily together is for them to spend "alone time" together in their various subgroups. Both partners must understand one another's need for "alone time" with their respective children and not interpret it as a snub. Equally important is time alone with the stepchildren in order to further develop some kind of bond. It might help to plan an activity that will entice them and give you something to talk about: movies, a sports event, a rock concert. Or it can be an activity as simple as a shopping expedition or a meal together—anything that will give you an opportunity to know one another.

My stepdaughter was 14 when I moved in, antagonistic and self-centered. I made a date with her once a week, just the two of us, to have a "girls' night out." I became her friend and coaxed her into counseling. She is close to me now and I love her a lot.

—Nancy, 49, consultant

The one advantage of being a single parent is the absence of child-rearing disputes which are commonplace even in very compatible marriages. A single parent becomes accustomed to making decisions without being questioned or criticized. But things may change dramatically with the arrival of a new spouse who brings opinions of his or her own on everything from the size of an allowance to the lateness of a curfew.

Many single parents admit to being too permissive. Thus, when they remarry, the most common disagreements are likely to be about discipline. Because they feel guilty about their divorce, they tend to bend over backward to make their child feel loved and accepted. They also fear that being stern will alienate the child altogether. As a result, single parents can easily be made the dupes of a manipulative offspring who plays one parent against the other. Also, they may be so overwhelmed by the job of supporting and raising a child alone that they can't muster the strength to be firm each time the situation calls for it.

I should have been stronger. I did all the cooking and cleaning. It was easier than asking my kid to participate and then listening to her whine. Much later, I finally gave her chores, which made her feel more responsible and more adult, more powerful and more important. I think she appreciated the structure, but I just didn't or couldn't do that earlier.

—Maggie, 54, lawyer

A stepparent needs to tread warily, however, even if it is apparent that the child needs stricter guidelines. He or she should think twice before being judgmental or critical, before volunteering opinions and advice, and certainly before stepping in as the disciplinarian, even if such intervention is justifiable and logical. For one thing, it takes time to build trust. Early in the relationship, a parent will probably have a subconscious, almost primitive tendency to protect his or her young from being harmed by a stranger. In addition, a newly remarried parent is likely to be somewhat nervous about how well a spouse will handle the job of stepparenting and how much the spouse can be trusted to do the right thing.

There was a lot of conflict. Every time he got agitated, I tried to calm him, and he'd say I was trying to protect [my daughter] and she was spoiled. And when he was direct with her, I'd jump in, and he'd say I shouldn't ask him to get involved if I were going to jump down his throat.

—Maggie, 54, lawyer

Not only is a parent likely to be defensive about criticism on behalf of the child, he or she may take it as a personal criticism. While all parents have some doubts about their parenting styles, single parents are much more likely to have misgivings and may attribute any of their children's missteps to the emotional problems caused by the divorce. Feeling guilty, the parent is probably hypersensitive.

Being hypersensitive may also cause a parent to be overly protective. Mom may see her unruly son as "the little clown," while his stepdad considers him a troublemaker with focus problems and the makings of a teenage delinquent. Or a stepmom may want to punish a teenager who flew into a rage and stayed out overnight while Dad says, "He's just acting like a kid."

I kept repeating the same stories to anyone who would listen for the first two years of my marriage, when my three teenage stepdaughters were unbearable. I would complain about [my husband's] lack of understanding of my situation. I would fume when he defended them and failed to notice how they were being nasty and obviously intended to hurt me. I was very unhappy because I hadn't expected this situation. Then I realized I had two choices: leave, or quit complaining and make it work. I chose the latter. But I had to make a definite plan and give myself weekly reminders. I knew I could not change their behavior, but I could gradually change mine. The most important thing was that I'd forgotten how much I loved this man and how much I wanted to be with him because I wasn't focusing on the love. I was focusing on the negative. I also realized that by accusing and pointing out the faults of his children, I'd left him no choice but to defend them. He was their father.

—Maryanne, 50, personal trainer

Everyone has to bend a little. The kids have to understand that all of you are coming together as a single unit, not simply living together as separate family groups under one roof, so you have to reach an accord. The adults have to understand the same thing. Instead of being defensive when the incoming spouse attempts to intervene, a parent has to think in positive terms about how helpful it might be to have the support of another adult in managing the children. Often, one person can step in and be stronger—and, on occasion, be even more compassionate—when the other person is having a difficult time. Chances are that the children will ultimately benefit in some way from the presence of a stepparent. Partners who are determined to make a success of their remarriage find a way to resolve their problems without being judgmental or critical.

Rivalry between stepparent and stepchild

A new stepparent may be surprised or even embarrassed by the emotions she or he feels.

I began criticizing my husband for taking his daughter to shop for clothes at a very fancy boutique. When I was her age, I was shopping at discount stores, and I just couldn't get over the idea of a 15-year-old wearing skirts that cost $300. I said that it was inappropriate for a child that age to have such expensive clothes, but the truth is, I was simply jealous. It's humiliating to admit this.

—Marlene, 28, teacher

When we first married, my husband and I went on ski trips every winter with my stepchildren. We don't get a lot of vacation time, and I resented the fact that we had only two weeks vacation together each year, and I spent one of them on the ski slopes. I don't like skiing—I don't even like the cold—and I resented the fact that my needs weren't a factor, and my husband was putting his relationship with the kids before his relationship with me.

—Leila, 45, fashion stylist

A stepparent may feel excluded from the parent-child relationship.

My spouse is having a hard time differentiating between the role of a stepfather and the role of the biological father. He says he feels like a "eunuch" because he doesn't have control over what happens to my daughter. Her father and I make the final decisions re: her going to camp, which college she'll ultimately attend, how we'll pay for her education, etc. My present husband and I are working on this issue in counseling.

—Sandra, 41, health care provider

My husband makes all the decisions, and the kids realize that I have no power in this equation. When he's not home, they completely ignore me. "I don't have to listen to you. You're not my parent." I want to be treated as someone whose vote counts.

—Marlene, 28, teacher

I feel as if I'm in the UN with a simultaneous interpreter. I say something, and my wife interprets it to her child.

—Howard, 52, printer

There may even be problems when the stepparent and child do bond.

I wouldn't have thought that I could be competing with my own child, but that's what happened. One weekend, she and her stepdad joined forces to tell me I was making too much of a thing out of keeping the house neat.

—Darcy, 45, interior decorator

"A man who is jealous of his wife's relationship with her own kids may line up with them against her to accuse her of being too controlling. What's really happening is that he's reacting to the fact that next to the kids he usually feels like a second fiddle. It's hard for a woman to present a 'united front' with her new husband in such circumstances," points out psychiatrist Scott Permesly.

In all these situations, the apparent problem is less significant than the underlying issue—which is that the stepparent and the child see one another as rivals. The child resents sharing the parent with a stranger—particularly if the parent and child have been very closely bonded in the type of quasi-emotional marriage described in Chapter 4. Clashes between stepparents and children of the same sex are more frequent than with children of the opposite sex because they are rivals for the attention of the opposite-sex parent.

In response, the stepparent may retreat. For his or her part, feeling abandoned and saddled with the burden of complete responsibility, the natural parent may become resentful and see the stepparent as acting in a childish way. This has two negative consequences. One, the more adversarial the stepparent and stepchild become, the more difficult it is for them to bond. And, two, it is destructive to the marital relationship.

Your goal is to act as coparents. Take the child out of the middle of the situation and agree upon a way to deal with the feelings of rivalry that have emerged. In a good marriage, the wife, for example, can say what is bothering her, and the husband will respond by saying, "I think you're misinterpreting," or, better, "I don't want you to feel that way," and go on to explain his view. Both people have to contribute to the discussion in order to come to some kind of resolution.

When a stepparent and stepchild are in competition, the stepparent is actually saying, "There's not enough love for me here"; "You don't love me enough"; "You're putting me second." In other words, "What about me?"

The spouses who are hearing such complaints have to understand their partners' need to be valued as much as the children; and the spouses who are making the complaints have to understand that the parents' need to take care of their children doesn't diminish their love for their spouses. If they can't come to an understanding, the parental partner may simply walk away.

I broke up with my second wife because she was too competitive with the affection I gave my son. The stepparenting stuff got in the way of the relationship.

—Ray, 55, abuse counselor

However, with some perspective—and, if necessary, some counseling—remarried adults can solve these problems and come to compromise positions that make them both comfortable. Accommodation like this sets a great example for the children.

In the early years of our marriage, competition for my affection was a big issue. I felt torn and guilty no matter what I did. Blended families require patience and unconditional love from both spouses.

—Lola, 45, claims adjuster

Problems unique to the "half-blended family"

In a half-blended family, one parent has custody and the other does not. One parent's biological kids live with the ex-spouse and the other parent's kids live with the new couple.

No matter what his inclinations and intentions are about remaining in contact with his biological children, the noncustodial parent (usually a father) will inevitably play a less significant parenting role for his own kids. His position is usurped by the residential stepparent, who is on hand to witness the daily milestones and offer comfort in the face of tribulations, to make policy on bedtimes and participate in doing homework, to pin on the prom corsage, run to the emergency room, and cheer on a sports triumph. It's hard to give credit, even harder not to feel jealous.

A nonresidential parent has to accept a lesser role in his child's upbringing. He can't always exert his will and taste to influence a child's development. Even though he may observe behavior and attitudes that he doesn't approve of, he'll have to reconcile himself to the fact that he can't change them.

A man (or woman) in this position must try to make sure his remarriage doesn't suffer as a result. Being apart from his own children, he is likely to overstate their good qualities and minimize their shortcomings when comparing them to the stepchildren. He may become excessively demanding of his new family. In addition, his guilt about abandoning his own kids may make him reluctant to spend time nurturing a family that is not his own. He also may be resentful that his ex-wife isn't giving his children the good mothering that he sees his stepchildren getting, and he may take this out on the stepchildren.

Dueling dads and defensive moms

Stepfathers may have a harder time than stepmoms. Aside from the guilt they may feel at "abandoning" their own children to raise someone else's family, being compared to the biological parent may be more of an issue simply because men are innately competitive. Fathers may vie to be the favorites. The "Disneyland Dad" is usually the biological, noncustodial father (though a stepfather may compete with the biological dad in this very way). The "Disneyland Dad" isn't necessarily rich, but he can provide at least some treats—more, no doubt, than he would provide if he were with the kids regularly. It's not that he's so generous: He's motivated by guilt and sadness. After all, he's not with the kids for many of their most important moments.

It's an unhappy situation all around. A stepfather who is less successful than the biological father may feel uncomfortable because his spouse and her children have come down in the world with the remarriage. A biological father may be resentful of the economic success of a new stepfather. This constant tension is a strain on the remarriage.

I went into this marriage with my eyes open. I knew we wouldn't have the financial advantages my previous husband could offer, but I really felt my second man was a better person and could teach my kids about virtues that were a lot more important to me than whether we had the latest model car or where we went on vacation. But you know testosterone. I guess he got competitive. He began to make snide remarks about my ex, and the net result was that [the remarks] made him look bad. I finally mustered up my courage and told him how I felt and why I had married him. I think it made him feel good to have my feelings for him reaffirmed, and he let go of the competition.

—Sarah, 45, guidance counselor

If one dad (or stepdad) plies the kids with treats, the children may feel guilty about succumbing to them, feeling disloyal to the other dad. And the situation may be nettlesome for a wife who sees her husband being manipulated (to spend more money) or shamed (because he can't compete). What gets lost in all the competition is the fact that spending a lot of money on a child doesn't help a parent build a real relationship. Playing with toys isn't as gratifying as having a conversation with a concerned parent who is focused on you.

A spouse can help think of ways the less affluent parent can involve the kids with experiences that cost little or no money. For example, parents who have skills in a sport might spend time coaching a child (and at the same time building their relationship) or taking the child on sports excursions. With an older child, they may be able to think of contacts who could offer entrée to a place or event that might be of special interest: a backstage visit, a part-time job, and so on.

Women are likely to have an easier time than men in a remarriage. The husband's children usually live with his ex-wife and so they may carry less guilt about the breakup of the marriage. Also, caring for a nonbiological child may come more easily to a woman than a man. On the other hand, a stepmother who isn't comfortable as a nurturer—a role she may be expected to fill—may draw a lot of criticism. And criticism about how the household and family are managed is generally directed against a woman rather than a man. The situation may be especially tricky if Dad is a widower. The more you're like the mom who died, the easier things may be. But if you're very much unlike her, or if in death Mom became a saint, you will have to take things very slowly.

There are gray areas where the stepparent's role is unclear. For example, if the child is having problems in school, who addresses them if the child lives with parents on alternate weeks or with one parent only on the weekends? Sometimes you just have to be guided by what you feel is in the best interests of the child and hope it all works out.

My husband's daughter had some behavioral issues at age 12. The school reported that she was getting in fights and pulling kids' hair. Her mother just shrugged off the complaints because she doesn't really want to be bothered. My husband was concerned, but he's not very good at dealing with psychological issues. I decided to step in because the child needed an ally and some help. Fortunately, the mother didn't really protest and, ultimately, my husband was very grateful to have me help out. I felt better because, instead of just criticizing the girl, who was acting out at home as well, I was doing something to help. Still, it was awkward, and I don't know what I would have done if the mother had been more resistant to my interference.

—Danielle, 50, restaurateur

A woman's version of being "Disneyland Dad" is being the perfect stepmom to visiting stepchildren. She won't try to buy the kids' affection; more likely, she'll try to get it by making everything perfect. But her efforts will probably go unrecognized and unacknowledged. She's better off not trying so hard.

I would ask my husband ahead of time what the plan was, when they were coming, and what he expected of me. He used to say, "I'll just order pizza," and I would think I couldn't do that, so I'd cook a gourmet meal. Then I would get mad when no one said a word about the meal and no one helped me clean up. I realized I was doing that to myself, it was my own agenda, and I didn't have to. Now I don't object when he orders pizza, and I am not resentful.

—Maryanne, 50, personal trainer

The house divided

When kids from two families live together, you can deal with them in three ways: You can treat everyone equally, which is impractical and doesn't always happen even in an intact family. You can bend over backward to do things for the stepkids, which is unfair and will make your children angry. Or you can favor your own kids, which may be normal but can cause a Civil War-type situation.

Instead, tell the children that you will do some things that will probably seem unfair at first but, as you get to know them, you may modify or relax the rules. (And make sure to follow through.)

They will need some guidelines in the most critical areas. Time is one of them: Which parents are going to be with which kids when and whose demands take precedence in case of conflicts? Space is another: What are the rules regarding chores, property, and privacy? Who gets what room?

Don't be surprised to find that any changes you make are unwelcome, at least initially.

We were in the house my husband had with his first wife. After three years, since his children were no longer there, we decided to convert one of the bedrooms into a dining room. When the son came home from his senior year in college for a visit, he took a look at what we'd done; then when his father went upstairs for a moment, he bent down and said in my ear, "You've taken away my bedroom." I said nothing and didn't tell my husband because it would have hurt him. I only mentioned it years later.

—Sami, 68, stand-up comedienne

Some of the problems are just a resistance to taking orders from an interloper.

There haven't been any major problems, but it's an ongoing thing— their relationship with their stepfather. They flat out say that it's nothing personal, it's that he's not really their dad. And that it isn't going to change. They are all dealing with that in some degree or another.

—Barb, 45, nurse

The biggest stumbling blocks, however, are the issues that push emotional and psychological buttons—most typically, in the areas of discipline and boundaries.

Whose standards apply?

When you form a stepfamily, you have to first decide what the rules are and then how you will enforce them.

It is only normal for people to believe that the way they are accustomed to doing things is the right way. If a stepparent was raised to value order and neatness, and a stepchild was raised in a family that didn't put a high priority on staying tidy and cleaning up after oneself, the stepchild is going to have a hard time following rules that he or she may not quite understand.

I felt it was difficult for the kids. They had two sets of parents (his ex-wife remarried) with two sets of values.

—Kyla, 47, journalist

It is understandable that a child might become confused when he or she alternates between two homes with different rules, and more confused still if there is a difference of managerial opinion inside the homes.

My former wife was raised in a home where the top priority was speed, and that's how she raised the kids. But my second wife is a scientist, and it's important to her that things be orderly. In her home, if you didn't make the bed correctly, you had to keep redoing it until you got it right. It drove her crazy when my kids came to visit and everything landed on the floor. They considered her standards pretty strange but, even if they tried to please her, they didn't know how to meet them. A family counselor told us to pick our fights—that is, decide which battles were worth fighting, and which would be better off forgotten. Finally, my wife agreed that if the kids left the room a mess while they were visiting, she'd just keep the door closed. Then, when they vacated to go home for the week, they had to do a more careful job tidying up. Both of them still think the other is excessive, but since they only had to clean up once a weekend, the kids didn't resent it so much, and my wife learned to deal with the closed-door weekends.

—Lloyd, 58, botanist

My spouse's ex is extremely permissive with their children. The 16-year-old son is very reserved and studious but the 14-year-old daughter is extroverted and rebellious. She is allowed to intervene in any conversation, volunteer her opinion whether or not it is asked for, go out whenever she wants without asking permission, and even have her boyfriend stay in her room overnight. I have a 12-year-old son and felt that this was not the behavior example I wanted for my child. I was extremely fortunate that my spouse felt that his ex-wife was too permissive and we had a family talk where we told the children what was permissible in our house and what was not. They had a choice to accept it or not. If they chose not to abide by our rules, they could not live with us. My stepdaughter decided to live with her mother but has now requested that she would like to move in with us. Her mother has changed and become less permissive. We allowed her to move in with us at the end of the school year.

—Marise, 42, consultant

Kids don't need identical rearing or loving. They need individual loving and rearing. But especially when you are mixing different parental systems, you need consistency in your home.

Being a parent or a role-model stepparent is an eighteen-year commitment to be consistent. Inconsistency, whether it comes from drugs or alcohol abuse or simply poor stepparenting skills, results in mental ill-

ness. Consistency and firm boundaries produce mental health and pre-
dictability, which allows a good flow between members of blended
families.

—Lynda, 54, therapist

One big problem is that people don't simply disagree about the rules, they also have strong feelings about whose rules are superior.

Through counseling we realized that no matter where children are in
life, they're going to run into situations where there will be different
rules. Just because the rules are different doesn't mean they are wrong.

—Penny, 45, child care provider

People living under the same roof may have different opinions in every area, from chores to bedtimes, neatness to table manners. For example, do kids clear the table? Must they remain in place until the meal is over? If they don't like what you're serving, can they get something else? You might think you are a participant in Middle East peace talks.

But you can't solve all the issues at once. For starters, you might want to talk about what chores the children are responsible for, the family guidelines for respectful behavior, who handles the discipline, and what kind of discipline is appropriate. You may have to modify the rules over time, but kids ought to know what they are.

Include older children in the discussions about rules to give them a sense of having a voice, and incorporate their suggestions as much as you can. But don't let them divide and conquer. Kids will try to do this as yet another ploy in their campaign to get their old family back. It's you two against them. They're younger and stronger and may outnumber you. Also, they're armed with those time-honored kids' tools, whining and badgering, which are amazingly effective.

I don't understand why he sometimes chooses his children's side over mine. His younger daughter will report a conversation to her father totally out of context. My husband knows I am a fair and honest person, and I think he has to give me some priorities.

—Marlene, 28, teacher

Your strategy is to build your team first. Negotiate between your-selves outside the kids' hearing so that the stepparent in particular won't seem like the "bad guy."

My husband never interferes between the kids and me. Any advice about my relations with them is always offered when they are not around.

—Louise, 60, dietitian

You will have a much easier time when the kids believe you are pre-senting a united front.

I sensed that the kids were more than happy to play everyone against the other, and finally my wife and I sat down with them, laid out the rules, and said that if they had any problems, they had both of us to answer to.

—Dan, 42, accountant

Defining the stepparent's role

A stepparent should ease slowly into the parental role to make the adjustment as easy as possible.

My spouse spent a great deal of time and effort on my children. He started out trying to win them over from the first. And even though they were teenagers, they responded. Once he had their trust, they didn't resent his occasional laying down the law.

—Louise, 60, dietitian

My husband left his wife, and I was very much unlike her, which meant the kids weren't exactly ready to welcome me with open arms. I thought it was more important to become their friendly housemate before I became the hands-on mom. I sort of let the kids guide me in figuring out how much of a mom they wanted.

—Rebecca, 36, sales

Most of the people we surveyed agreed it was best not to start out trying to be the disciplinarian. Clearly, sounding critical or nagging should be avoided.

Stepmothers often have a harder time in this area. Explains Scott Permesly, "Often a man fights for custody of his children not so much because he wants the responsibility of raising them but because he hates the first wife. Then, when he gets them, it falls to the stepmother to manage the domestic areas. She may get into trouble when she imposes rules and regulations in an attempt to get the household to run smoothly."

The biggest issues of our marriage were always about disciplining the children. Weekend fathers don't like to discipline their children, ever. They just want to entertain them because they feel tremendous guilt. So I would have to be the disciplinarian and then I would be the guilty one. We would endlessly discuss the fact that I didn't want to be seen as a tyrant and, at the same time, I knew the kids had to have boundaries.

—Kyla, 47, journalist

"For things to work out in a household like this, and to avoid stepmom taking all the heat, Dad has to take over the discipline," Permesly says. But also it should be made clear to the kids that when the stepparent is alone, she or he is the one in charge, and that the two of you have made this decision together.

Although children of a divorce almost always have a hard time accepting the authority of a stepparent, at least initially, in the end stepparents and children usually find ways to settle down comfortably together.

We had agreed to discuss every discipline issue before we decided how to hand out punishment, but that just wasn't practical. Inevitably there were times when one of us was coming down on the other's child and there were issues. So then we decided we'd punish our own kids, which was completely crazy, but we didn't know what else to do. What finally brought it to a head was when my daughter forgot to lock the front door and my wife lost her temper. But when she saw how upset my daughter looked, my wife gave her a hug and said, "Emily, I know this will sound weird to you, but the reason I'm reacting to this is because I really do care about you." It was really from the heart, and that seemed to help move things along to the point of real acceptance.

—Dan, 59, photographer

In our case, we disagreed about certain things, so finally this is what I said, "Your mom may do the disciplining around here, but there are some things I will not put up with," and I spelled them out. I also told them that I might have to add to the list as things came along. I didn't want to be an ogre, but it was a strain for me to bring all my complaints to my wife. Ultimately, I don't think the kids reacted as much as she was afraid they would. They're used to school rules, sports rules, and so on, and they know that sometimes different rules apply. Also, I was careful to tell them what I had to at a point when I wasn't mad.

—Jack, 65, lawyer

Boundary issues

Children make constant and all-inclusive demands and invade both your physical and psychic space, so there's a constant need to set boundaries. In the biological family, these boundaries may be implicit. But when a new family is formed, you may have to spell them out.

How much censorship and control will you exercise over the children? At what age may they sit with you while you are watching films made for grown-ups? What parietal rules are in force when high-school friends visit or when college students return home with dates who are staying overnight?

How much privacy does everyone expect? Are children invited to come into the parental bedroom whenever they wish or will the door be locked? Does the "knock before entering" rule apply to the kids' rooms, too? And which of the following are considered unacceptable violations of privacy: reading one another's mail, picking up one another's answering machine messages, reading one another's e-mail?

My husband's grown daughters routinely came into the bedroom to borrow his clothes. But now it wasn't just their father's bedroom—it was also my bedroom they were coming into. I wasn't used to having a 22-year-old woman coming into my private space and looking through my closet or going into my medicine cabinet. My own daughter did it because she'd grown up with me, but this was different. I had to explain to my husband that I just wasn't comfortable with an open-door policy to our bedroom. If the girls wanted something, they had to ask for it and let us get it.

—Lois, 41, realtor

If it's truly an item like a piece of clothing—or simply attention—that the children want, they'll be satisfied if you give it to them. However, their actions may reveal more if you look deeper. In the case above, it might be that the children like the stepparent's style and/or see her as more glamorous than their own mom, and by going through her things, they are really trying to figure out how to emulate her. Or they may be trying to steal back what they feel belongs to them. If you can figure out what's going on, it may bother you less, or you may be able to find a way to deal with it.

Relationships between step-siblings

People often don't focus on how the children will get along with each other until after the marriage, and more often than not it turns out to be a minor issue. Believe it or not, if you're lucky, the kids will decide to join forces to work in concert against the parents. That's because both sets of kids will discover that they resent their respective parents for the very same reasons.

An only child may benefit from, and even enjoy, having siblings once he or she gets over the initial shock of not being treated preferentially.

My new wife's son was an only child and he truly didn't seem to get the fact that there were "kid duties," "kid responsibilities," and "kid limits" along with "kid privileges." In other words, you had to do the former before you earned the latter and, in any case, children never had the same rights as their parents. At first, he chafed at doing chores, and finally we just made a work schedule. That stopped the arguments. Though he didn't always carry out his responsibilities on time or with great goodwill, at least he knew what he was supposed to be doing because it was right there in black and white. The schedule also helped my kids see we were being fair in terms of the amount of work apportioned out to each kid. The older kids had more to do, but we figured it would take them less time.

—Howard, 52, printer

Competition within stepfamilies

If, in one set of stepchildren, certain roles are already established— "the smart one," "the responsible one"—it may be difficult for the stepchildren on the other side to feel special.

Similar problems may arise if one set of stepchildren consistently does better in school, is more popular, more athletic, and/or more attractive than the other.

A difference in values between the two families may set up an unpleasant rivalry. If the new stepfather is an athlete and his step-son prefers to read or *vice versa,* a child may be criticized either for not venturing onto the athletic field or for never reading a book.

Any of these situations has the potential to pit not only the children but also the adults against one another. This is a case in which parents have to be very sensitive to each other's feelings as well as those of the children. Parents have to deal with these situations as they do with any sibling rivalries, only more cautiously, because in a sense the parents may become rivals, too. Help the children develop skills in particular areas; if necessary and possible, put them in different schools, camps, and other situations, and seek professional help.

Sexuality and the stepfamily

Adolescents, especially, because they have a heightened sense of sexuality, may have problems dealing with some of these issues when they move in with a stepparent and/or step-siblings of the opposite sex. For one thing, this "new" family hasn't gone through a process of familiarization. And for another, parents in a remarriage may be more ardent and their sexuality more public than is customary in a long-term marriage.

Kids may handle their feelings in strange ways. They may even compete with a parent and begin to flirt with the stepparent. If a child seems to be behaving inappropriately, a parent has to set boundaries. "What might be normal in a nuclear family—a daughter coming in and sitting on her parents' bed and talking to them at night; a son coming in when his mother is in a nightgown next to a man—may not feel right in a remarriage," says therapist Roxanne Permesly. "You have to make certain rules that are discussed ahead of time. Meet with the kids alone and meet with your spouse alone. Tell the kids that they have to knock, that you're not comfortable with them walking around in their underwear. Put a lock on the bedroom door if you have to."

It's not unusual for stepsiblings to be sexually attracted to one another. Since they are not related biologically and because they probably don't see each other regularly, the incest taboo may not be in place. Sometimes step-siblings of opposite sexes have violent arguments; this may be bcause they fight their feelings of attraction.

You may feel that you're in over your head in trying to handle problems in this area; if so, get some help.

When stepkids come to visit

Years ago, Anna Freud suggested that after a divorce a child should stop seeing the noncustodial parent—in effect, have his or her own divorce from that person. Painful as it would be, this might sometimes seem like a good idea to people facing the difficult issues that arise when stepkids come to visit. From the very moment the children are handed over to the noncustodial parent for a visit there may be problems all around.

The two former spouses may have trouble being polite to one another. The custodial parent may be anxious about relinquishing responsibility for the child, and the other parent may resent what he or she sees as excessive attempts to stay in control.

Again, the most common situation is one in which children leave their mom's house, where they normally live, to visit their dad and stepmom. The stepmom may be uncomfortable with the amount of time her husband spends with his ex to arrange these visits, concerned about how the kids will respond to her, and guilty because she really wants them to be gone so she can have her home, time, and spouse all to herself. While the stepchildren are there, she will probably be expected to treat them as guests. If they fight with the residential kids she may have to mediate between them. She'll also have to refrain from commenting on the amount of time, money, or energy being lavished on them or from criticizing their behavior.

I don't know how I got through those visits from the stepkids. They were so badly behaved that every time we took them out, I wanted to wear a tee shirt that said, "None of these children is any blood relation to me."

—Emma, 51, producer

A noncustodial father will have his own problems during a visit. He may try to make up for his prolonged separation by cramming many experiences into a short period of time, pampering and spoiling the children, and relaxing the discipline—in part out of guilt and in part in an effort to make things go smoothly. However, he may be thrown by behavior he's never seen when the kids start relaxing their "best behavior" and become noncompliant or defiant, or squabble with one another. At that point his instincts to "get those kids back into shape" may conflict with his desire to protect them from the criticism of the stepparent.

Or the father may surrender the responsibility for taking care of the children to his new wife and go off and play golf. "The stepmother doesn't like it, and neither do the kids. What I hear in therapy is, 'Dad used to be so much fun until he married this woman; we used to order pizza for dinner and sit on his bed, eat popcorn, watch TV and stay up late, and now she won't let us,' " says Roxanne Permesly.

Children have plenty of their own expectations regarding the visit. They may arrive with the fantasy that life will be better with the noncustodial parent. Or the ex-spouse may have conditioned them to hate their dad and his current wife, and they may feel that any show of appreciation or enthusiasm will be disloyal to the custodial parent. The resident children may resent being physically and emotionally displaced by the visitors, and the visiting stepchildren may resent the resident children for having taken their rightful place with their parent.

It was very painful for my kids to see their father with other children, to see him playing ball with kids when he hadn't done it with them.
—Debbie, 58, social worker

Step-siblings may ignore one another or be openly hostile.

Given all these points of conflict, the remarried couple is very likely to quarrel between themselves about favoritism and discipline. They need to prepare for visits with discussions in which they form actual plans. While the biological parent should not foist the stepparent on the children, the stepparent should be included in some of the plans as an active participant so he or she is less likely to feel like an invisible host or housekeeper. Also, it might help to come to an understanding that the children are visitors rather than integral members of the family unit. Perhaps that will encourage everyone to be more tolerant and reduce the amount of urgency around the issues that arise.

My stepchildren come for a month each summer (along with the occasional winter holidays), and things have been much easier with them since I took the advice of a friend of mine who has four grandchildren. When they come to visit, she lets them stay up late, eat junk food, and watch violent cartoons on television. She figures that the kids understand that the rules at her house are different and that the parents will get them back in line when they go home. I decided that rather than be nagging all the time, we could do the same: make the kids happy and reduce the stress by relaxing the rules and being a little less strict than either my husband or I would normally be. We figured my husband's ex-wife would probably find fault with whatever we were doing anyway.
—Carla, 46, advertising copywriter

For three years, I was "camp director" for my visiting stepdaughter and my husband would go off to work. Then I realized the best thing was to distance myself. I decided that I would visit my parents when my stepdaughter came. My husband didn't want to come with me on those trips anyway, and he had the obligation to be with his child. But this way, no one was taking it personally: It wasn't that the child got the message "Vicki doesn't want to be with me," but simply "Vicki can't be here." This worked for everyone.

—Vicki, 40, music teacher

Dealing with "family events"

"Our cultural forms, rituals, and assumptions still relate chiefly to the intact, first marriage family, and the most ordinary event, such as filling out a form or celebrating a holiday, can become a source of acute embarrassment or discomfort for members of remarried families," writes Elizabeth Carter, ACSW, in material distributed by the Stepfamily Foundation.

When you're in a remarriage situation, it's hard to take the kids "over the river and through the woods to grandmother's house," because there may well be four grandmothers vying for a visit (and all of them are probably not through the woods but in Florida!). The joy of graduations, weddings, and Thanksgiving celebrations can be diminished and the grief of funerals can be exacerbated when families disagree about details: who should be invited, where they should be allowed to sit, even whether the sweet potatoes should have a marshmallow topping.

You may be able to negotiate a settlement, but you can't enter an institution assuming you can change it. If the family has "always" spent vacations on Long Beach Island or "always" gone to Grandma Springer's house for vacation, you may have a lot of trouble making other plans.

An old Yiddish saying—"With one behind, you can't dance at two weddings"—comes to mind when you're a remarried person dealing with the holidays. You're forced to choose. Whose relatives do you spend them with? Whose house should be considered headquarters? Like all the other situations involving the megafamily, diplomacy is required. Sometimes people in a second marriage take the simple approach to overcoming fixed ideas about how the holidays should be spent. They decide it's their life, and their Thanksgiving (or Christmas, or whatever), and whoever wants to join them can do so. Or they blaze a new trail.

We tried being with my husband's children some years and with my kids the alternate years, but then my kids would be upset because their father had nowhere to go. Finally we worked out the perfect solution. My husband spends the holidays with his kids, and my ex-husband and I get together with our kids in some neutral place, like a restaurant. When our children get married, I guess things will get more complicated still, but this is a surprisingly happy arrangement all around for the moment.

—Lauren, 55, human resources director

Since the underlying purpose of many of these events is for the children to feel they are cared for, it is up to the adults to work out some kind of compromise that puts them first. That's why many parents have worked out arrangements in which each couple visits for half of a camp visiting day or half of a college Parents' Weekend. It's not the most satisfactory arrangement, but it's often the best solution.

Finding your way

There is no one solution for every family. The remarried families to whom we spoke have worked out various kinds of accommodations.

DON'T GO ON THE ATTACK

I have had some experience with Twelve-Step programs and I think that helped me figure out how to communicate with my new husband about family issues that were difficult. You have to make yourself the subject under discussion. Don't say, "Your daughter did [such and such]." Then the daughter is the issue. And don't say, "You aren't dealing with your child's [whatever]," because then your spouse feels attacked and is dealing with issues of his own self-esteem. Make the subject of the sentence "I." Train yourself to make "I" statements. You may be conveying the same information, but you're doing it in a way that it's more likely to be heard. "I feel scared when I see your daughter do [whatever it is]," or "I feel uncomfortable when I see your son [act in a particular way]," or "I am upset by doing [things in a particular way] because it's not what I am used to." Yes, it's possible that the response will be, "I don't give a damn." But if that's so, you have to question what kind of a marriage you're in.

—Danielle, 50, restaurateur

WORK ON PROBLEM-SOLVING SKILLS

As mentioned in Chapter 6, Florida has mandatory courses in co-parenting for spouses who are divorcing. In Massachusetts, divorcing parents with children under the age of 18 must go separately to a two-session, five-hour sensitivity training course called PACT (Parents and Children in Transition) run by a team of both men and women and developed with the help of a committee made up of attorneys and psychologists. Similar mandatory programs also exist in Arizona, Connecticut, Delaware, Iowa, Minnesota, and Utah and are in the works in other states.

One of the goals of the course is to help parents recognize and avoid behavior that can be emotionally traumatic to children. This includes having arguments and fights in front of the children, using the children to carry messages between hostile ex-spouses, and exposing the children to casual dating too soon after the divorce.

Perhaps the most useful tool that the parents learn is a technique called "reflective listening." This is a useful device to ease tension and it can pave the way to finding solutions through discussion.

1. **Listen and attend**. Concentrate totally on what the child is saying. Stop whatever you're doing and focus your attention.

2. **Understand and accept feelings.** When the child is telling you how he or she feels—"I hate Dad"—don't deny those feelings by saying, either directly or obliquely, "No, you don't."

3. **Rephrase and reflect feelings.** "You sound angry/hurt/as if you're feeling left out."

4. **Listen again.**

PATIENCE PAYS OFF

Remarried couples can work as a team to make the family be what they both want.

My husband saw that my teenage daughter needed fathering, but he said he didn't want to do it. At one point, we [sent her to live] with her father for a while. Before she returned, we got together and rewrote the rules at my therapist's suggestion. All of us were there: my ex and his wife, and me and my husband. We made rules about curfews, responsibility, even doing the laundry and other chores. Before that, it was playtime over at [my ex-husband's] house and he never imposed the rules, but this time he and I agreed that whatever I said, went. By then he was probably tired of her too. This time she knew we meant business. The meeting cleared the air, let us see each other differently, and gave us a chance to complain. At first my daughter was the least willing of all of us to comply, but she came around.

—Maggie, 54, lawyer

I definitely wanted a home with kids in it. It was part of my life plan to have a world that expanded beyond the workday. My former wife felt she had put in her time with the kids and although I didn't exactly understand her position, I was absolutely content with it. I respected my new wife's skills as a parent. Having already raised some kids, she wasn't looking to practice being the "total mom," and she was confident about her role. When some of the kids took a little longer to warm up to her, she never got hypersensitive. She knew that was how kids act. By now, the kids are all fairly tight with her. I think anyone who is about to stepparent teenagers ought to read every book out there, check in with therapists and join support groups to help them get through it.

—Andy, 58, architect

I found it so useful to talk to other people about all these issues. I never had kids before and I was taking everything personally and feeling I had joined this completely dysfunctional family. One of the kids wore a headset practically twenty-four hours a day. Another one wanted to pierce his tongue! And then I'd compare notes with coworkers and it turned out that my stepkids weren't all that different from their kids, and they didn't think things were so bad.

—Yvonne, 42, accountant

VENT—SORT OF

I went to a lecture on stepfamilies and the person speaking suggested that since so many people have a hard time expressing their anger and irritation and staying on top of things, they should write letters to their partners. Then she gave the "rules" for writing the letter:

1) *You do not have to be fair.*
2) *You do not have to be nice.*
3) *You do not have to be right.*
4) *You do not have to be polite.*

Of course, I was bowled over. I was thinking, "What kind of people can send each other letters like this and keep the marriage intact?" And then she gave the fifth rule:

5) You may not send the letter.

She explained that one purpose of the letter, of course, is to let out all of the anger. No matter what you've said to your partner in anger, there's a whole lot more—because you do have a shred of decency in you—that you've kept to yourself.

And then she explained that it had an even greater therapeutic value. She talked about a study of depressed people who were not getting medication. One third of the group was told to keep a journal of their feelings, a third saw a therapist regularly, and a third was a control group that was given no direction. The last group was generally un-changed but the journal-keepers and those who were seeing therapists improved at about the same rate.

Like visiting a therapist, keeping a journal gives you a chance to ventilate and explore your thoughts. So I decided to try keeping a jour-nal, and it's true that when I read back over it, say a month or so later, I found that a lot of it was pretty silly. There were many, many things that I could really let go of. And it became clearer to me which issues were really important to me. Best of all, I had my thoughts more to-gether on what exactly it was that bothered me, and I could bring them up and discuss them much more rationally.

The really important thing, though, is to hide that journal where no *one can find it!*

—Danielle, 50, restaurateur

KEEP SOME RESPECTFUL DISTANCE

This stepmom backed off a little and was very successful in building her relationship with her stepchildren little by little, over time.

I didn't expect to be an instant mom to his kid. But I think I have played a really significant role in their lives that is meaningful to all of us. I could be a sort of Auntie Mame, not in terms of spoiling the children with indulgences but by being indulgent in the sense that I wasn't emotionally involved. When either one would fight with their dad and stormed off, I could knock on the door and try to explain his behavior. Sometimes I was able to persuade my husband that his daughter was, indeed, old enough to wear makeup, or that his son's behavior wasn't weird based on what I knew of kids and remembered from my own childhood. When my stepdaughter decided to drop out of college for a year, which was a blow to her parents, I realized that she was actually making the right decision based on who she was. (She eventually returned to school, older and wiser about she wanted.) I was much more detached, and I think the kids really benefited. Sometimes it helps to be a disinterested outsider.

—Joelle, 56, painter

The children resented their stepfather at first, but when they realized that he loves them as well as me, they became closer and closer to him. Their father never had enough time for them. They learned from this man that love means time, affection, and even discipline. They, and I, know that he is a very special man.

—Lizbeth, 28, clerical worker

In my case, the mother had died unexpectedly and it was very hard on the children. At first, my husband had difficulty getting everyone together. But a year after we started dating, my younger stepson took me aside and said, "Thank you for making our father so happy."

—Sally, 43, office manager

KEEP FOCUSED ON YOUR MARRIAGE

"One good thing about second marriages is that children may not dominate the relationship as they sometimes do in first marriages. The first time around you're likely to become so engrossed in being a parent that you lose the 'couple' element of your relationship. Men especially like to feel that they are part of the couple—that Mr. and Mrs. So-and-So exist as an entity apart from the children," says Rox-anne Permesly.

My feeling is, my child will be gone at 18. I hope that my husband will be with me for a long, long time. I see many marriages where everything revolves around the child and the husband becomes the nonentity. In our home, we eat when my husband wants to eat. If my daughter can't wait that long, I sit down with her and prepare something for her, but I want to have dinner with my husband. It's a constant challenge, be-cause there are times I have to tell my daughter that I'm going off to travel with my husband and she doesn't like it. But it's a big mistake not to travel with your husband. On the few occasions when I can't possibly do it, I make sure we have a great night of sex before he goes. I want him to go away happy.

—Tara, 36, housewife

The bottom line is that, no matter how much the children may complicate the situation, the success of the stepfamily, like the success of the remarriage itself, rests on the adults: how respectful, kind, and considerate they can be to one another, and how serious they are about making the remarriage work.

STAY WITH IT

No matter how unresolvable the problems may seem, if you are determined to find solutions and are patient, they will come.

"I tell my patients that when they work together to solve their problems, they're teaching their kids," says therapist Judith Siegel. "By creating the example of a loving, supporting union in their re-marriage, they're giving their children a gift. It is a model that children can emulate in their own life and one that is especially important if it's been preceded by a conflictual marriage. It can be a win-win prop-osition."

When I married at 21, I was busy overriding my own wants and needs in favor of traditional expectations. At 39 I had resolved much of this, though six or seven years into marriage number two I did seek counseling because I was angry and ready to jump ship again. We had custody of his three children, and they were generally good to me; the problem was mainly with me. I really was not prepared to accept all the usual adolescent trauma, including having to appear in court a couple of times when they really pulled a bad one. No one in my own family has ever gotten more than a traffic ticket. I wanted more control than the normal teenager allows, and this was a great source of frustration. Counseling helped me to refocus and reprioritize, and subsequently my husband and I engaged in marriage counseling as well. All this has helped me to gain enough distance from myself/ourselves to be able to understand and resolve problems. We have an improved ability to resolve problems which continue to occur. Each time we do come to a resolution, we have learned something new, and this is very rewarding and satisfying.

—Olivia, 53, horse trainer

It's no small miracle when these situations work out. It takes a lot of patience and maturity from the adults. However, time has helped to settle our situation, and I am very proud of all three of my stepchildren. They have bonded with my son, their new little brother, and have a true working relationship. I admire my stepdaughters, and we have become good, caring friends. My stepson and I have mutual respect. We have overcome a lot of problems and are building a relationship so we can overcome whatever else our lives have in store.

—Hannah, 34, government worker

WHY REMARRIAGES SUCCEED

I'm deliriously happy in my remarriage. In my first marriage, I was merely delirious.

—Philip, 53, photographer

Making the commitment to marry is an act of courage. If it's companionship you're after, you could simply date. That's much easier than making a binding emotional, psychological, and legal pledge to be responsible to another human being.

Committing to a remarriage takes even more courage. Someone who pledges fidelity, respect, and the other obligations marriages entail for a second time is usually much more aware of the compromises and work that is involved. But he or she goes ahead and does it anyway. Marriage, after all, is deeply rooted in our psyches as the traditional, inevitable, and consummate act of a caring relationship.

I felt, if you love somebody, you get married. After a year of dating I began feeling awkward about how I would be introduced. Being a "girlfriend" was okay for a sweet young thing in her twenties. I was over 40. I didn't feel comfortable saying to hell with convention, either. I felt, for myself morally and in my conscience, that I wanted to be married, to know exactly where I was in life, rather than floating like an orb on its outskirts.

—Roberta, 53, government secretary

After dating for four years, I felt [marrying her] was the right thing to do. That would add stability to my relationship and to my family. There has to be an end to a story. Either marry or end it.

—Ira, 48, lawyer

I'm a physician and, professionally, it's impractical and socially awkward not to be married. I didn't like going to a medical conference and introducing the woman I was with as my "friend."

—Douglas, 56, oncologist

Things were great when we were living together. I was a little fearful that marriage would alter our relationship for the worse, but my husband is socially conservative and he pressed for it. Actually, things have gotten better because he became far more relaxed.

—Kendra, 52, executive director

Though most people we talked to seem to have gone into a first marriage feeling extremely uncertain of themselves and unclear of their goals, happily remarried couples had been thoughtful and confident about making their choice.

The first time I married I was young and thought the man would fill my every need and that magic would occur and we would live happily ever after. I never thought about focusing on my personal goals.

—Kathryn, 48, public relations executive

Before my first marriage, I was unsure, sad, [and] scared, and my feeling was, "Oh, well . . ." This time, I was excited and anxious, but also very calm and sure of myself.

—Elaine, 43, tour guide

The night before my first marriage, I knew I didn't really want to get married, but I didn't have the nerve to cancel it. It was a marriage based more on lust than love. This time around, I had no doubts whatsoever. We had so many things in common.

—Erica, 34, clerical worker

Often, as a benefit of aging and experience, people are less influenced by what they believe they should do, so they operate more from instinct and what "feels right." Thanks to this effect or to counseling or a combination of the two, many mature people have figured out what it takes to make a marriage work and dedicate themselves to making it happen.

Before I married my present wife, I thought about everything more. I saw things that I respected. She was a single mother, she was working, she was pursuing her career. She was committed, focused, ambitious, liked her relationship with her own parents, and was very caring. The first time I married, I wasn't thinking, "What are your values?" I wasn't thinking about anything. I don't even know why I got married.

—Wally, 58, architect

Prior to my previous marriage, I had several concerns relating to our ways of dealing with emotional issues. My second marriage, however, is based on mature love, communication, and respect. All issues that could have been problematic had been discussed ahead of time. I went into it without any apprehension, but with a sense of profound joy at having had the chance to have met someone as wonderful as my second spouse.

—Marise, 42, consultant

In the first marriage, these people were marrying someone who filled the role of "spouse." In the second, they were connecting to a particular individual.

Settling into a remarriage

Of course, marrying a second time's not necessarily easy. Even though you may have more maturity and experience, the first year or two of a remarriage may be as difficult as the first year of a primary marriage. You may have forgotten some of the lessons you learned—that the period of courtship and the process of falling in love are not exactly like "real life." During courtship, people are on their best behavior. And when you are falling in love, you tend to be blind to your beloved's flaws. In the initial period of attraction, you project onto one another all the qualities you desire.

Nobody's perfect. No matter how carefully you've considered the pros and cons of making a marital commitment, you sometimes tend to overlook what it will be like when you're lost on a car trip and he refuses to get directions; when she's forgotten to pick up your shirts at the laundry; when he's losing his temper over your kid's minor infraction; when she thinks you're overreacting to something her mother said—when, in short, you each will discover that the other person is sometimes stubborn, irresponsible, impatient, and insensitive, or lacking in some other way. At some point, you have to decide whether you're going to stay with this imperfect person or pull up stakes again and move on.

If you belatedly discover that a partner has a completely unacceptable trait, goal, habit, or deficiency, you'll probably exit quickly. But if you have chosen your partner well, the good qualities will far outweigh the bad, and you will stay in the marriage. Most likely, you learned from your first marriage that just because you love someone, you don't necessarily love everything about that person, nor do you find them lovable all the time. Even the most charming and attractive of people may have irritating habits, unpleasant moods, and bad hair days.

"My impression is that in a first marriage, even if a person was unhappy with the choice of a spouse, many people learn what is special and to be valued about being married," says therapist Judith Siegel. "Subsequently, they may be willing to work a little harder to preserve the institution. This means you don't take it lightly. You shift your priorities. You are perhaps more sensitive to a partner and more willing to compromise out of respect for the idea of marriage."

Those who "hang in there" will still have a great deal to work through. Love songs to the contrary, two people can never come together as one. The older you are, the harder it is to compromise, because the older you get, the more opinions you have. You like blue, he likes green; you like birch and glass, he likes mahogany and leather.

Some 20 percent of men and 9.6 percent of women we surveyed felt first marriages and remarriages were equally difficult, while 40 percent of men and 33.3 percent of women felt remarriages were easier.

Most participants, however—40 percent of men and a substantial 57.1 percent of women—felt that a remarriage, at least initially, was more complicated than a first marriage.

Remarriage is very hard work.

—Juliet, 47, teacher

Marriage is always a give-and-take situation. There are three factors that seem to determine if it will last: how mature you are, how much you care for one another, and how good you are at compromise. The process of working out your differences is not always easy, but the fact that you have a common goal may bring you closer than you might have imagined.

My first husband and I had a deep love, but it was a young love. This time what we have is a mature love. It has a balance that my relationship didn't have in the past. This husband doesn't have a fiery temper. If we have problems, we talk things out. I guess this is what happens when you get a little older. I'm so appreciative of this relationship.

—Esther, 49, singer

The effort to compromise is well worth it. "A loving marriage helps us to grow in special ways we can't do alone. Intimacy is a challenge. It forces us to recognize things about ourselves that we otherwise might miss. A second marriage can help heal some hurts from the past by helping us to understand those issues and help one another work through them," says family therapist Audrey Wentworth, herself the veteran of a remarriage.

It wasn't easy in the beginning, but over the first three years of our remarriage, a lot of the problems have diminished.

—Hannah, 34, government worker

When we talked to people who had been in therapy before they married, some very significant factors emerged. Although 57 percent of women and 51 percent of men had seen a counselor in a prior marriage, only 17 percent and 24 percent of them respectively felt it was helpful. In the current marriage, 35 percent and 16 percent had seen a counselor, and 74 percent and 60 percent respectively believed it helped. Perhaps the prior experience suggests why the marriage didn't work; being in therapy requires a willingness and openness to communicate and work. One might speculate that, in their second marriage, the partners were more receptive to counseling because they were more determined to make the marriage work, and thus found it more helpful.

The reasons for a happier remarriage

Why were our survey participants so much happier than in their past marriages? Two of the reasons had to do with changed external circumstances. Forty-two percent of both men and women indicated that they were in an improved financial situation. Six percent of the women said they were happier because they had a job. The fact that the children were off on their own was cited by 18 percent of men and 12 percent of women.

But most of the reasons why these men and women were happier in a second marriage had to do with personal growth. The percentages below show how people accounted for a marriage that was more successful than the one that preceded it.

	Women	Men
More self-esteem	62	33
More compatibility	73	69
Better companionship	54	49
More mature	71	43

That 41 percent of the women and 49 percent of the men also said that the sex was better is surely connected to a higher level of compatibility.

"Within individuals who have a happy second marriage, a shift has taken place. It may be a shift in identity, expectations, the degree to which they have a realistic perception of the world, or their way of thinking. The shift is from negative to positive," says psychotherapist Jill Muir Sukenick.

"A first marriage may be characterized by a less developed sense of self with infantile needs and interactions taking precedence. A second marriage brings out a healthier selfishness and a less masochistic selflessness. You know how to ask for what you want, yet understand that there are limitations, sacrifices, and compromises," Sukenick explains.

Leo Tolstoy, the novelist, wrote that "Happy families are all alike." In speaking with happily remarried people of every age and background, we discovered that successful remarriages are very much alike as well.

They have many characteristics in common, each of which, as Sukenick suggests, represents a negative-to-positive shift:

from being self-effacing to being self-confident and independent;
from having inappropriate, or uncertain, criteria to having a clear sense of one's own partnership needs;
from holding vague or immature notions to truly understanding the realities of marriage;
from being closed off or isolated to having the tools and willingness to communicate;
from being sexually inexperienced and selfish to being self-aware, empathic, and generous;
from being egoistic and inflexible to being mutually respectful and tolerant;
from being shortsighted or thoughtless to holding long-term goals for the relationship;
from being indifferent or noncommittal to being determined to make marriage a success.

Assertiveness and self-awareness

Women, in particular, were likely to go into a first marriage with low self-esteem, especially if they were financially dependent. This meant they were often willing to take a secondary role in the marriage. But by the time they remarried, many had learned to assert themselves because the majority of them had been obliged to support themselves, and sometimes children as well (or at least to manage their affairs), and/or they had gone for therapeutic help.

They had learned that it is not a job requirement that a wife be totally submissive.

I didn't think of myself in my first marriage. I did what my mother did. I tried to make my husband happy.

            —Clara, 54, university administrator

In my first marriage, I was like a geisha girl. I wanted to make him happy. The problem with that kind of relationship is that the moment you stop giving that kind of attention, your spouse goes out to find someone who will.

            —Marcy, 37, designer

I thought if my husband and I got a divorce, my world would come to an end. He was the most important thing about my life. I was devoted to being a good mother, a good wife; it was a twenty-four-hour-a-day job. But I learned that the commitment has to come from both sides. I lost myself. I lost my identity and who I was.

            —Samantha, 52, retail manager

I was 21 before the first marriage, and 39 at the time of my second. At 21, I was busy overriding my own wants and needs in favor of traditional expectations. At 39, I had resolved much of this.

            —Olivia, 53, horse trainer

In my first marriage, I made hors d'oeuvres to serve before dinner, and I put on eyeliner every night before I went to sleep. I thought otherwise he'd divorce me. I thought I had to be the perfect wife and I got angrier and angrier. I kept it all in. This time, I can say what I feel. I told him

I don't like cooking. That doesn't make me a bad wife. He told me that he understood how I felt because he had been married twice before, and he was angry too. None of us realized you could ask for things. You could say, This is who I am, and this is what I want. You don't have to feel guilty.

—Roslyn, 55, book editor

Judith Siegel says, "In *Lasting Marriages*, Richard A. MacKey and Bernard A. O'Brien talk about the very feelings these men and women are expressing when they discuss the concept of authenticity. Couples in a first marriage often marry into a role that sometimes traps them. Rather than assert themselves they act according to some notion of how they ought to act. And instead of entering into conflict, they will hold their feelings in and not be authentic about who they are or what they want. This unresolved conflict is extremely destructive to a marriage."

After that first marriage, they learned the importance of satisfying their own desires.

You need to consider yourself first. If you don't know what you want, you can't possibly figure out what you want out of a relationship.

—Norma, 46, beauty salon owner

I realized it's not his job to make me happy. It's my job to make me happy.

—Becky, 52, graphic designer

Before my first marriage, I did not like myself a whole lot. I was still trying to please Mommy and Daddy, not living my own life. I was much happier with myself prior to my second marriage.

—Ruth, 25, data entry clerk

My second husband was more experienced. He said, "Your problem is with how you regard the institution of marriage." And that kind of helped clarify things for me. I didn't want to be dominated. I didn't need a parent. And I learned that a marriage partner didn't have to be that.

—Rosalind, 48, court reporter

My happiness does not depend on my having him in my life. I always pursue my own goals.

—Vicki, 40, music teacher

They discovered the reservoirs of their strength.

The first time I was looking for someone to save me. It took me a long time to realize that I didn't need to be saved and I didn't want to be.

—Donna, 50, management consultant

In the eight years following my first marriage, I grew very strong and knew I didn't have to be married again. I learned I could keep my kids going and I learned self-appreciation.

—Sami, 68, stand-up comedienne

I had my own life and my own goals, which would remain the same whether I was married or single.

—Kathryn, 48, public relations executive

And the pleasures of being self-reliant became clear.

I felt I was more in control of my mind and my body. I was thinner. I had a better sense of style. I had a career. In my first marriage, I wasn't even expecting to work.

—Helen, 58, writer

After I was single, I enjoyed regaining my independence and making my own decisions. I didn't realize how much I missed that. I learned to enjoy life again. I learned that I would never allow myself to give up my freedom again—it was too important to me.

—Katherine, 46, stockbroker

They developed the confidence to become more intimate.

When I married the first time, I had no clue who I was or what subconscious feelings were motivating my behavior. As I came to understand my choices and why I had taken the path I had, it became easier for me to make different and healthier choices. That in turn has allowed me to feel more comfortable and confident within my own skin, and allows me to let others, especially my husband, be more fully themselves. (At least on good days, that's how it works!)

—Juliet, 47, teacher

And the second time around, they made marriages of choice, not necessity.

I have higher self-esteem now. I know I do not have to stay married to survive, which to me means that I am where I am because I want to be—not because I have to be.

—Penny, 45, child care provider

At age 23, I was dependent on my husband for most things in my life. I understand what an adult relationship is now.

—Kate, 51, actress

I am an equal partner in this marriage, and I was not in the first one.

—Louise, 60, dietitian

My outlook is that this is the best time of my life—so much better than when I was younger and trying to figure out who I was.

—Frank, 59, real estate agent

Having a sense of one's partnership needs

It is not sufficient to be chosen: To make a happy marriage, you too must choose.

I didn't think anyone would want to marry me, so when my first husband proposed, I just accepted. When I married my current husband, I knew what I wanted in a mate and was not willing to settle for anything else.

—Janet, 33, housewife

This time around, I looked for someone who would care about my needs and see that some of what I wanted would get done. That didn't happen in my first marriage.

—Beth, 53, office manager

I wanted a wife who had an identity as a working person. My first wife had a law degree but she quit work to take care of me and our son. I'd come home and she'd be talking about some new recipe she'd made. I wanted someone who wasn't waiting at home to hear about my day, somebody who had some news of her own to report.

—Burton, 53, lawyer

I divorced her because I didn't want to be married to someone whose only goal was to be Mrs. Him.

—Frank, 57, therapist

The people who were in satisfying remarriages had put a lot of thought into what they expected in a partner. They weren't interested in superficial qualities but looked for personality traits that would help ensure a good relationship.

After my divorce, I'd been in therapy. I made a list of the qualities I wanted in a man. I carried this list with me. When I went back to a high-school reunion—in part because I wanted to strike up a reacquaintance with an old boyfriend—I brought the list along. When I looked at the list, I realized he fit every category: someone who took his family seriously, who would be a good father, a good listener, and who could support my work.

—Cyndi, 45, artist

Between my first marriage and the time I met my second husband, I had grown a lot. I was more specific about what I wanted in a man: someone honest, loyal, and true, someone who worked hard and had strong beliefs and family values.

—Angela, 33, customer service representative

He was good, kind, reliable—and it was apparent that I could be top dog in this marriage, be anything I wanted, and he would support it. I knew that was what I needed. I look back and think, "Boy, was I a calculating bitch," but in fact I made a smart, great marriage.

—Barbara, 46, personnel specialist

The second time, I was looking for a man with ambition, a man closer to what my father was like, a man who was not going to feel he had to teach me. I wanted to be more of an equal partner.

—Helen, 58, writer

The first time I was a dumb kid who married the first pretty girl who would do it with me. I was twenty years old and head over heels in love. But this time around, I had the list.

—Louis, 46, small business owner

The experience of being in a marriage that fails teaches you to avoid certain types of negative behavior.

My first husband was sexy, exciting, macho. We were in a glamorous business and led an unusual life. But he cheated on me. I chose a second husband who was very stable and predictable and intelligent. If you were making a list of all the people who might fool around, it wouldn't include him.

—Barbara, 46, personnel specialist

I looked for someone who wouldn't be another stay-at-home, dependent ex-wife. My present wife is independent and educated, she has her own business and her own money. I would not get back in the same situation as the first time.

—Ira, 48, lawyer

Understanding the realities of marriage

Who hasn't indulged in magical thinking from time to time, fantasizing about meeting the perfect stranger with whom you'll find unconditional love and lasting marriage? Fortunately, most people understand that in real life, that kind of giving doesn't just happen; love is thoughtful, not thoughtless; it requires dedication and effort.

Getting married for the first time was [a case of] going along with the times and still doing what we were expected to do by our parents and peers. But with no knowledge of what to expect it was like jumping into a black hole. I married my second husband after four years of dating. I was more aware of what can happen in a marriage. I was sure of my love for him. Being older and mature, and with the knowledge that nothing is perfect, I made my decision to marry him. We were committed to the fact that there probably would be problems but we would work them through. I know the pain of divorce and I don't want to go down that road again. I made this marriage because I wanted and chose it, not to please anyone else.

—Leigh Anne, 39, business owner

By the time I got remarried, I was ready to stay married. I waited till I met the man I wanted to spend my life with.

—Rita, 45, college professor

When you get more mature, you know you have good days and bad days. You don't need a Valentine's gift every year.

—Lauren, 55, human resources director

Being able to communicate

In *The Pleasure Bond*, sex therapists William Masters and Virginia Johnson say that communication—"with or without words"—is the most important component of a second marriage. The couple keeps the marriage alive, Masters and Johnson say, "as long as they [understand] the importance of communicating, of keeping in touch, of constantly making the effort to reach out."

With maturity and experience, you learn that love doesn't have to be expressed as it is in the poetry on a valentine.

In my first marriage, I overlooked the real signs of love: The fact that he was there for me, that he took over so many of the household jobs, that he was responsible and giving. I thought I needed to hear the words. That was a big mistake. I was foolish. Fortunately, when a second good man came around, I'd been single long enough and learned enough to understand that love is expressed by what you do, perhaps even more than what you say.

—Helen, 58, writer

Many an "odd couple"—people with superficial differences—get along fine when they are responsive to each other's emotional needs. One such couple that springs immediately to mind are Mary Matalin and her husband, James Carville, who helped run the campaigns for opposing political parties when George Bush and Bill Clinton were vying for the presidency. Seeing eye to eye on politics or any other topic is not as important as having an attentive and responsive partner.

She would be telling me about her work and I wouldn't hear a word she said. I would tell her about my work and she wouldn't hear a word I said. We just didn't care. We were each hung up on what we were doing separately. After 18 years I came home one day and she said, "We're done." I was totally shocked. I was thinking, "What's her problem? We have all these things. *" But she needed someone to tell her he loved her and that he cared. She left me for a pool cleaner who had nothing but a pickup truck. But he had more to offer than I did. He had time. He had time to appreciate her.*

—Burt, 46, engineer

Many a happily remarried person described a current spouse as a "soul mate" or "my best friend." And though you can communicate feelings nonverbally, you need words as well.

In my second marriage, we can talk about anything. I didn't realize a marriage could be like this, because I was so lost and alone in the first one.

—Haley, 54, headhunter

In a successful marriage, it's not only important to be able to speak openly and honestly about your feelings, but also to listen and understand what your partner says. Speaking the same language isn't the same as communicating. *That's Not What I'm Saying* by Deborah Tannen and *Men Are from Mars, Women Are from Venus* by John Grey are two of many books that have attempted to explain the difficulties men and women have understanding one another.

Generally, women are guided by the left-hand part of the brain, where feelings dominate, and men are right-brain thinkers who are guided primarily by logic and reason. Right-brain thinkers deal with problems by taking action. "Let's work out a solution," they'll say, or "What can I do to help." This "logical" approach helps them distance themselves from their feelings. Women may have better access to their feelings but have trouble putting them into words or demanding a response; and they may also fear being labeled too emotional. Feeling obliged to squelch their feelings, disappointed by the insufficient or inadequate responses from their partners, they may become bored, angry, depressed and even self-destructive—a pattern that is often seen in an unhappy first marriage. Acknowledging what is going on is a giant step forward.

I'm primarily a feelings type person, and my darling likes to "live in his head" and use his intellect to try to solve problems, discounting his feelings; this was stressful for us both, and even caused him some physical problems. We are both learning to share and validate what our bodies are telling us, and working to use each other's strengths and be aware of what mode we are employing and why. It makes for a good balance. We are always surprising each other with insights based on our orientation. It's fun.

—Wynona, 49, teacher

People may become physically intimate quickly and comfortably and yet have a great deal of difficulty becoming intimate about their thoughts. But if they can't communicate by talking, eventually physical communication may become unsatisfactory or impossible. What characterizes a happy second marriage and sets it apart from the first is that the partners have both the desire and ability to talk frankly:

I know communication is an overused word, but unless you can make your feelings known, you won't make much progress. You can have the greatest sex in the world, but eventually you have to climb out of bed. You have to be able to understand other. Being able to talk honestly about things that bother you is important. But the other side of talking is listening. That's probably the most powerful thing you bring into the relationship.

—Roberta, 53, government secretary

I am more likely to express my opinions and desires than in my previous marriage. My new spouse is more open in that regard and more sensitive.

—Rebecca, 36, sales

I have some of the same problems as in my first marriage—I think I'm hard to live with—but at least this time, my husband speaks up. I admit that sometimes it hurts my feelings, but it helps.

—Maggie, 54, lawyer

When you see that something's going on, don't wait for your partner to come to you. As soon as I see my new wife is quiet, I ask, "Honey, what's wrong?" If she says, "Nothing," I insist on talking to find out what the problem is.

—Burt, 46, engineer

Neither of you should fear the consequences of speaking freely.

We worked on how to handle each other without just getting angry and upset. We would say, "You know how much I love you and I would never want to hurt you. If I say something that hurts you, before you get angry, let's talk about it, because it's probably not what I intended to do. Give the benefit of the doubt before you lose your temper and walk away." If he does something that really hurts my feelings, before I get really angry and upset, I try to say to myself that I know he wouldn't intentionally hurt me so let me stop a minute before I think the worst. Most of the time, it works.

—Marcy, 37, designer

The more you talk, the more you get past the notion of perfection and start dealing with the real human being you fell in love with. The closeness you develop helps you make a bond strong enough to hold you together through the stresses that may push you apart.

Being sexually self-aware and empathic

In a remarriage where there are children, intimate moments may be less frequent and less spontaneous than in a first marriage. We cherish the idea that romance happens "naturally" but mature partners leading more complicated lives may have to give a little extra thought to keeping passion in the relationship and finding opportunities for closeness. A husband and wife who care about satisfying each other's needs for intimacy will work actively to find solutions, even in a less-than-ideal situation.

The secret to our remarriage happiness is taking time for each other. We hug each other and hold on for a long time. We call just to say, "I love you." We still go on dates at least one to two times per month. We talk and we cuddle, even if it is on the couch covered with kids.

—Ivy, 28, housewife

Being with someone older, you may have to work even harder. I'm twenty years younger than my husband and I have to deal with the things that happen to men as they age. I want him to feel like he's a wonderful lover even though he's always scared he's going to have a heart attack every time he has sex. You have to work at the sexual side of the relationship. Every day. Twenty-four hours a day. It's a respon-

sibility, but it's also like a game: How do I make things more exciting? Otherwise the sex gets boring. It can't possibly stay the same as when you first started dating. Make time and take an afternoon together. Skinny-dip in the pool. Wear something provocative. Whether or not you actually have sex, you're making your husband feel good. More important, you feel good about doing your part.

—Tara, 36, housewife

"A man's sex life may take on a new dimension as he gives up the compulsion to insist on penetration for amorous satisfaction and learns to accept and enjoy caressing initiated by his wife," writes Eleanor Hamilton, a retired psychologist and sex therapist.

My husband is on the road a lot, sometimes for two weeks at a time. When he returns, I am very interested in getting physical. Sometimes the feeling is mutual, but sometimes it's not. I had trouble accepting this. He told me that he loves me very much, and he always wants me, but that he doesn't have to have sex to love me. The problem is that my husband thought that having intercourse is the only way to express yourself sexually. He really didn't understand the idea of caressing, holding, touching, kissing. He thought if you kiss, you have to have sex. We worked on that, and it did help. Now we can kiss and touch (even pet) without it leading to sexual intercourse. This was a breakthrough for us. We are determined that our marriage will work. I love my husband; I love him with all my heart. The differences we have are not enough to break up our marriage.

—Erica, 34, clerical worker

Of course, the effect of Viagra on sexual relations is not to be discounted.

Without the sex, I believe it's very difficult to make a relationship work. I describe it as the warmth in the relationship. And now that we've got that little blue pill, kiddo. . . .

—Malcolm, 55, editor

Older couples have found it very liberating sexually to be past the child-raising years. There's less to fight about, they have more opportunity for privacy, and of course they no longer need to be concerned about unwanted pregnancies.

If a young married couple won't use contraceptives for religious reasons, it causes all kinds of pressures and problems. Most couples come together in the bedroom, but if you can only have sex when it's safe, because you've been taught it's a sin to use contraceptives, it takes a toll over twenty or thirty years. In my final analysis that was the major cause for a lot of dissension and unhappiness in my first marriage.

—Jack, 65, lawyer

Remarried couples have found sexuality to be about more than sex.

Before my present relationship, I thought sex was the most important thing. Now I don't think about it so much because I have all the love and affection I could possibly want or need out of the bedroom, which makes the sex like an extra treat!

—Nancy, 49, consultant

EPILOGUE: THE PLEASURES OF REMARRIAGE

The pleasant surprise of doing this survey was that so many people told us how happy they were in their second marriage. Despite any problems in the marriage, 42 percent of the women and 51 percent of the men said without reservation that, should this present marriage not work out, they would remarry. Nearly 11 percent of women and 13 percent of men said they probably would (if there were no children or interfering ex), and 24.4 percent and 15 percent respectively were not sure. Of the 22.6 percent of women who said they would not remarry (along with 21.1 percent of men), many went on to elaborate why, and a sampling of what they said follows.

Because I will never in this lifetime meet another individual like my husband.

—Ivy, 28, housewife

Because I don't believe love like this would be easy to find again.

—Rebecca, 36, sales

Because I'm so love with my husband.

—Rita, 45, college professor

Because I love this man too much, and I don't think I would ever find another that could begin to fill his shoes.

—Florence, 43, housewife

Because I would want only the memory of this marriage, since no man could ever compare.

—Elaine, 43, tour guide

When asked, "What is the greatest source of pleasure in your re-marriage?" the people we talked to mentioned these qualities.

Fidelity:

Being with someone who loves me and supports me totally. Having someone be by my side and putting me first. My husband is always here for me.

—Annette, 48, health care professional

Intimacy:

We have great sex.

—Virginia, 77, retired

Compatibility:

We had the same goals about [where we wanted to be and what we wanted to do] together. We didn't want to be stuck in one place with one church and one school and one soccer field, and become the Waltons.

—Allison, 52, fashion designer

Affirmation:

The ability to know that someone is there for you and love you unconditionally. There's a wonderful comfort in knowing he will be home and we will have our times together, like even when we're busy and I sit on the bathroom floor and talk while he's shaving. He always has the right thing to say. Just little things, like when I feel I need a facelift and he says, "You look great, just like you did when I first met you." And he means it. And that's what it is for me, knowing I have that person there and he's my best friend.

—Donna, 50, management consultant

Companionship:

My wife is my partner and friend. She's not a trophy. She's my equal.

—Wally, 58, architect

Joy:

My chief pleasure is discovering how happy people who enjoy each other can be.

—Enid, 46, gallery owner

Passion:

I don't think people should marry for anything other than love. Love is the only enduring thing. It's what makes the cement. It's like beauty: You know it only when you see it. A guy in love at 50 is the same as a guy who falls in love at 16: You think the sun is brighter, the flowers are more beautiful and the birds sing more sweetly. Someone you're just having dinner with—well, it just isn't the same.

—Arthur, 79, executive

Endurance:

Still being in love, and I mean really *being in love, after eighteen years.*

—Louise, 60, dietitian

Devotion:

He said, "I will treat you so well it will be too hard for anyone to follow me."

—Miriam, 63, nurse

Support:

My husband takes care of me emotionally and physically. No matter how bad my health is or how many hospitals I'm in, he always is there with a reassuring smile and an "I love you." He's the best.

—Leslie, 46, hairdresser

Adoration:

About fifteen years ago, he asked me to stop cooking. I was horrified and asked if the problem was that he didn't like my cooking. (I am an excellent cook.) He said, no, that wasn't it; he just resented the time I had to spend in the kitchen. It would be so much nicer if we could just have dinner out in a beautiful restaurant and he could look at me across the table and not have to do dishes afterward. It is my great pleasure to know that I have this buddy, this man who makes my heart race every time he walks in the door. He is my lover and my sweetheart and my best friend and my mate forever and for all eternity and he should have the best of me all the time.

—Sami, 68, stand-up comedienne

Comfort:

That we both let our feelings be known, we communicate, I feel I can tell him everything, we can be open and honest with each other. We can both be ourselves. We both feel that each other is the *love of our lives and we let each other know it. We are comfortable with each other, but we also have excitement and passion.*

—Veronica, 37, caterer

Laughter:

Even if it's a difficult situation, we laugh. In my first marriage, I cried for twenty years.

—Anne, 63, real estate broker

Self-confidence:

I had very low self-esteem, felt worthless, and was thankful that anyone at all would have me before this marriage. Thanks to my current spouse, I now know that I am worthy of having the best, and I now feel equal to others, instead of below them.

—Lizbeth, 28, clerical worker

Affection:

There's nothing like having a companion, especially one you can nuzzle up to and like it.

—Jack, 65, lawyer

Loyalty:

He accepts me just as I am, and we have complete trust.

—Marie, 44, police officer

Self-respect:

My chief pleasure is pride in being married to someone I respect so much, knowing I am a better person with him than without him. Because he takes my fears away, he makes me a better person.

—Haley, 54, headhunter

Acceptance:

Just allowing yourselves to just be yourself with each other.

—Hank, 53, photographer

Fulfillment:

I consider my remarriage a celebration of fulfillment. I was single and loving that freedom and variety for fourteen years. Then I wanted more and I met my wife. I love her, our life together, the companionship, the sex. My second wife is completion and fruition for me. It's a more mature love and I want to grow old with her.

—Bill, 55, artist

For a second wife, a second life is full of promise.

INDEX